The Hummingbird Garden

Turning Your Garden, Window Box, or Backyard Into a Beautiful Home for Hummingbirds

by Mathew Tekulsky

Photographs by the author

Crown Publishers, Inc.
New York

Also by Mathew Tekulsky

THE BUTTERFLY GARDEN

Copyright © 1990 by Mathew Tekulsky

Published by Crown Publishers, Inc., 201 East 50th Street, New York, New York 10022

CROWN is a trademark of Crown Publishers, Inc.

Manufactured in the United States of America

Library of Congress Cataloging-in-Publication Data

Tekulsky, Mathew, 1954-
    The hummingbird garden : turning your garden, window box, or backyard into a beautiful home for hummingbirds / by Mathew Tekulsky.
        p.   cm.
    1. Hummingbirds—North America.   2. Birds, Attracting of.
1.   Title.
QL696.A558T45   1990
639.9'78899—dc20   89-27020
                                                                             CIP

ISBN 0-517-575485
10 9 8 7 6 5 4 3 2 1
First Edition

To my mother and father

Contents

Acknowledgments

I would like to thank the following people for being so generous with their time and expertise: Melanie Baer of the Theodore Payne Foundation for Wild Flowers and Native Plants; Kimball Garrett (Section of Ornithology) and Robert Gustafson (Section of Botany) at the Natural History Museum of Los Angeles County; David Hutchinson of the Seattle Audubon Society; Daryl Koutnik of the Los Angeles State and County Arboretum; Steven Sibley of the Cornell Laboratory of Ornithology; and Sheri Williamson of the Arizona Nature Conservancy. Thanks as well to the many other people who provided technical assistance to me during the writing of this book.

I would also like to thank the many hummingbird gardeners from across the country who were kind enough to tell me about their gardens. Special thanks to members of the Santa Monica Bay Audubon Society in this respect.

Thanks as well to my literary agent, Jane Jordan Browne, for her support and encouragement, and to my editor, Brandt Aymar, for his advice and direction.

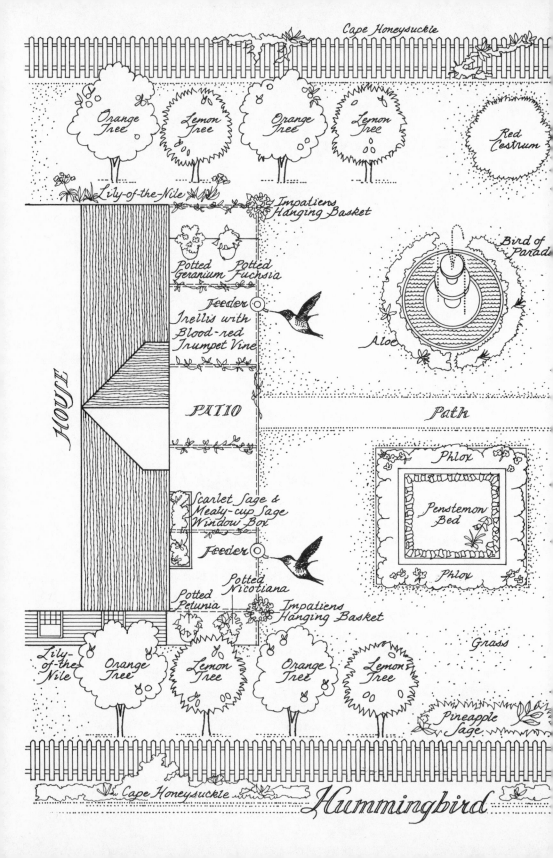

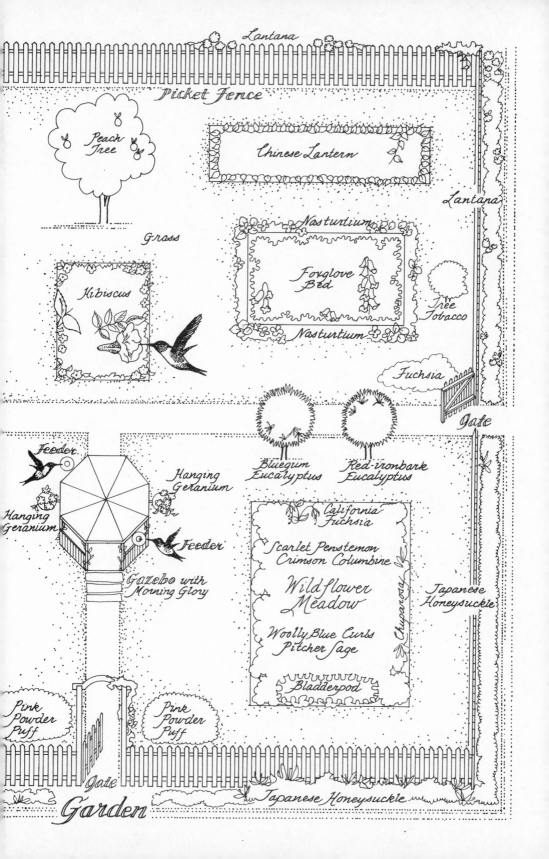

What Is Hummingbird Gardening?

~•~

I t is a calm, clear day, and you are standing in a garden that is designed to attract hummingbirds. All around you are flowers that provide nectar for these smallest of birds, which hover on fast-beating wings while they drink. An orange Cape honeysuckle covers a trellis on one side of the garden, while a blood-red trumpet vine does the same on the opposite side. A row of pink powder puff runs along the rear of the yard, and in each corner, a red-ironbark eucalyptus grows.

Behind the flower beds, a long stretch of pink Chinese lantern graces one side of the garden, while a row of yellow bladderpod blankets the other side. In the flower beds, the richly colored flowers of woolly blue curls grow side by side with the scarlet flowers of pitcher sage, penstemon, and columbine, while throughout the rest of the garden, the orange flowers of bird of paradise, the yellow flowers of tree tobacco, and the purple flowers of lantana can be seen. In front of the pink powder puff, a long strip of California fuchsia provides a three-foot-tall curtain of tubular red flowers for the hummingbirds to use.

Suddenly, you hear a familiar sound—the gentle humming of wings. In that same moment, a male Anna's Hummingbird is upon you, hovering in front of your face, just inches away. Hit at just the right angle by the sun's rays, the hummingbird flashes a shiny, metallic, ruby-red throat and crown at you, then looks away and the colors turn dark. The hummingbird, scarcely larger than your thumb, bobs up to one spot in thin air, then bobs over to another, turning his head toward you each time so that you are both eye-to-eye.

Satisfied that he knows who and what you are, the hummingbird darts over on a straight trajectory to a Chinese lantern bush, showing his iridescent green back as he bounces in midair from flower to flower. Then, content that he has finished his meal, he darts off, in another straight line, over the bladderpod and the Cape honeysuckle, disappearing from view just as quickly as he had arrived.

Perhaps nothing in all of nature deserves to be called a miracle as does the hummingbird. The smallest warm-blooded animal (along with the shrew), this tiny bird's metabolism is so high that the bird could not be any smaller than it is and still survive. And yet it frolics through the air as a dolphin does in water—totally at home in its environment. Indeed, the hummingbird can fly backward, forward, up, down, even upside down, thus making it the most proficient flier, despite its diminutive size, of all the birds. Perhaps only the fly and the bee are better aerobats than the hummingbird.

From the smallest hummingbird, the Bee Hummingbird (*Mellisuga helenae*) of Cuba at just two and one-quarter inches long from bill to tailtip, to the largest, the aptly named Giant Hummingbird (*Patagona gigas*) of South America, at eight and one-half inches in length, humans have been interested in, been intrigued with, and revered hummingbirds of many different shapes, colors, temperaments, and sizes, for as long as man and this remarkable bird have shared the same environment in the New World (the only place hummingbirds exist).

Since hummingbirds subsist primarily on the nectar that they glean from flowering plants, along with various types of insects that they catch in their bills, the relationship between hummingbirds and the flowers on which they feed is an intimate and an ancient one. (There are no fossil records of the fragile hummingbird, so no one knows exactly when it evolved.)

Through the ages, hummingbirds and their favorite flowers have been observed and celebrated in the legends of North and South American Indian tribes and in the recorded experiences of Europeans who explored and settled the New World.

One of these settlers, Governor John Winthrop of Connecticut, sent a hummingbird nest to a colleague in England in 1670, along with a note stating, " 'Tis an exceeding litle Bird, and only seen in Summer, and mostly in Gardens flying from flower to flower, sucking Hony out of the flowers as a Bee doth; as it flieth not lighting on the flower, but hovering over it, sucking with its long Bill a sweet substance."

Another early American, naturalist John Lawson, described the Rubythroat in his book *A New Voyage to Carolina,* published in 1709. "The Humming-Bird is the Miracle of all our wing'd Animals," Lawson states. "He is feather'd as a Bird, and gets his Living as the Bees, by sucking the Honey from each Flower."

In 1732, the close association between the Rubythroat and the tubular trumpet creeper (or trumpet flower) on which it feeds was depicted in both prose and an engraved plate by scientific illustrator Mark Catesby in his *Natural History of Carolina, Florida, and the Bahama Islands.*

"It [the hummingbird] receives its food from flowers, after the manner of bees," writes Catesby. "It so poises itself by the quick hovering of its wings, that it seems without motion in the air."

In 1825, at the "Beech Woods" plantation in West Feliciana, Louisiana, John James Audubon completed his original drawing of the Ruby-throated Hummingbird taking nectar from the trumpet creeper. Three years later, this drawing appeared in his classic work *The Birds of America.* In 1831, in Volume I of his *Ornithological Biography,* Audubon described his feelings as he watched the Rubythroat in the process of gathering nectar for itself:

"Where is the person who, on seeing this lovely little creature moving on humming winglets through the air, suspended as if by magic in it, flitting from one flower to another, with motions as graceful as they are light and airy, pursuing its course over our extensive continent, and yielding new delights wherever it is seen;—who, on observing this glittering fragment of the rainbow, would not pause, admire, and instantly turn his mind with reverence toward the Almighty Creator, the wonders of whose hand we at every step discover, and of whose sublime conceptions we everywhere observe the manifestations in his admirable system of creation?—There breathes not such a person; so kindly have we all been blessed with that intuitive and noble feeling—admiration!"

The trumpet creeper still blooms at Mill Grove, Audubon's first American home, by the side of Perkiomen Creek in eastern Pennsylvania, as it no doubt did while Audubon lived on this farm in the early 1800s.

Now an Audubon Wildlife Sanctuary in the town that bears the artist's name, Mill Grove also has some other plants that hummingbirds like, including butterfly bush, butterfly weed, cardinal flower, coral bells, salvia, and jewelweed.

According to Alan Gehret, assistant curator, the cardinal flower, butterfly weed, and jewelweed are all native to this part of Pennsylvania, as is the trumpet creeper, and all of these flowers were probably present during Audubon's days here.

The blood-red trumpet vine (a close relative of the trumpet creeper), along with numerous other hummingbird plants, blooms at the Pacific Palisades home of humorist Will Rogers, which is now a California State Historic Park. Here, the house and gardens remain as Rogers left them, and Anna's Hummingbirds still nest and nectar in the eucalyptus trees out back and visit the lantana, century plant, acacia, red cestrum, bird of paradise, and other flowers planted in beds around the house, in addition to the blood-red trumpet vine that runs along a trellis on the north wing, above the patio between the two wings of the house, and even on the chimney.

Will Rogers no doubt had many opportunities to witness the various habits and antics of the hummingbirds at his home. The pleasure of experiencing the visits of hummingbirds to one's garden can likewise be enjoyed by anyone who takes just a little bit of time and effort to provide hummingbirds with the flowers they need to survive. Where the flowers are, so will be the hummingbirds.

As Alexander F. Skutch states in his gem of a book, *The Life of the Hummingbird,* "Let a man plant a flower garden almost anywhere from Canada to Argentina and Chile, in the lowlands or mountains, amid humid forests or in irrigated deserts, and before long his bright blossoms will be visited by a tiny, glittering creature that hovers before them with wings vibrated into twin halos while it sucks their sweet nectar."

Indeed, whether you live in the country, the suburbs, or the city; whether your garden is in the mountains, on the desert, or by the seashore; whether you reside in Florida or Alaska, southern California or Maine, you can plant a wide variety of common garden plants, wildflowers, shrubs, vines, and trees whose flowers provide nectar for the hummingbirds that migrate to or are residents of the North American continent north of Mexico. The same principles, of course, can be applied throughout Central and South America, with the hummingbirds and flowers that are common in those regions.

According to Paul Johnsgard, in his book *The Hummingbirds of North America,* there are 342 species of hummingbirds in the world. Closely related to the swifts (they share the same order, Apodiformes), hummingbirds have their own family, Trochilidae. Of the 19 hummingbird species that occur in the United States, 15 breed here regularly; however, only one, the Ruby-throated, occurs in the eastern portion of the country.

Throughout the rest of the Western Hemisphere, and increasing in number and diversity of species the closer one gets to the equator (Ecuador has 163 hummingbird species alone!), there is an incredible variety in shapes, colors, and sizes of hummingbirds. For instance, in South America, the White-tipped Sicklebill *(Eutoxeres aquila)* has a sickle-shaped bill that fits perfectly into the curved blossom of the flowers on which it feeds, while the Sword-billed Hummingbird *(Ensifera ensifera)* has a bill that is longer than its entire body and is specially adapted to fit into the long tubes of the flowers on which it feeds, to the exclusion of other hummingbirds.

But perhaps the most remarkable-looking hummingbird in the world is the aptly named Marvelous Spatuletail or Marvelous Hummingbird *(Loddigesia mirabilis)* of Peru. Photographer and hummingbird expert Crawford H. Greenewalt writes in the July 1966 issue of *National Geographic,* "When I saw the living bird, I could hardly believe my eyes. The museum skin, impressive as it was, had not prepared me for the dazzling beauty of this superb and unusual creature."

Indeed, the Marvelous Spatuletail, unlike any other bird, has only four tail feathers, two of which are fan-tipped, extend in long, hairlike appendages two or three times the length of the bird, and can be crossed while the bird is perching, lifted over the bird's head in a mating display, or extended to each side during its stretching exercises in the morning.

No North American hummingbird has the particular physical attributes of the Marvelous Spatuletail, but each species of hummingbird that visits or resides in our region is unique and extraordinary, as close observations of these remarkable birds will indicate.

This, then, is one of the benefits of creating a garden that will attract hummingbirds—to be able to see the hummingbirds whenever you like. Whether it is the Calliope Hummingbird (the smallest hummingbird that breeds north of Mexico), with the beautiful scarlet streaks on its throat; the Costa's Hummingbird, with its striking violet throat and crown; or the Anna's Hummingbird, with its sparkling red throat and crown; the shiny iridescence that hummingbirds exude when the sun hits different parts of their bodies at a certain angle can provide hours of viewing enjoyment in and of itself.

But the behavior and antics of hummingbirds are equally intriguing to watch, preferably within the confines of your own garden. Since all hummingbirds are territorial and protect their nesting, nectaring, and perching sites with extreme vigor and diligence, you may at any moment witness a male or a female hummingbird chasing an intruder away from a favorite nectar source, perch, or nesting area. When this happens, the two birds (one following closely behind the other and chipping wildly) may buzz by, within a few feet or even inches of your head at twenty-five to thirty miles an hour, disappearing over the nearest hedge. A few moments later, the victorious male will return and treat himself to his much-deserved nectar from his favorite plant; or, if it's a female that did the chasing, she may return to make sure that her nesting area is okay, and then she may reward herself right away with some nectar from her favorite flowers.

Hummingbirds must have prodigious memories, for they are known to return to the same nesting and nectaring sites year after year. In time, you may get to know the hummingbirds in your garden as individuals, even as families.

Margaret L. Bodine did. Writing of her "holidays with hummingbirds" in the June 1928 issue of *National Geographic*, she describes with charm and enthusiasm the regular visits of Ruby-throated Hummingbirds to a second-story porch at her summer home in Maine. Covered with a clematis vine, and well-stocked with flower boxes, the porch area also featured numerous small bottles that Bodine filled with sugar water for her hummingbird visitors and attached to stems and hanging perches in the window area of the porch. From this vantage point, she could observe the intimate details of hummingbird life, from a mother feeding her young by jabbing her beak down the baby's throat (this is normal feeding behavior) to a hovering female licking some of the sugar water from a person's finger.

But perhaps the most charming of Bodine's recollections is her story about "Crazy Jane," a female hummingbird who "won her sobriquet because she insisted on drinking the overflow of syrup from the bottom of the bottle, where it ran down on the outside, instead of from the top, as did all her fellows."

Perhaps this anecdote lies at the heart of what attracting hummingbirds to your garden is all about. I've spent many hours in the field and in gardens, observing hummingbirds and their behavior, and from all of this fieldwork, one thing has become abundantly clear—they never cease to amaze me. Just when I think I have figured them out and know all there is to know about some aspect of their behavior, and so predict their movements and activities, they do the complete opposite of what I had expected them to do—or perhaps they do something totally new (at least to me) altogether.

For instance, I had been observing a number of male and female Anna's Hummingbirds taking nectar from a large patch of south- and west-facing Chinese lantern bushes at a corner house just three blocks from where I live in the Brentwood section of Los Angeles (see Photo 1). Although bird of paradise, azaleas, daylilies, and orange and lemon trees—all recognized hummingbird flowers—were readily available across the street to the south and west, I never saw the hummingbirds taking nectar from the flowers of these plants. Aside from a nearby bottlebrush and an acacia tree in which the female no doubt had a nest (for she always returned to it eventually), all of the hummingbirds at this site spent most of their nectaring time at the Chinese lantern bushes.

Although this was interesting enough to me by itself, it was only after I developed some photographs of the hummingbirds taking nectar from the Chinese lantern (and I use the word "from" advisedly, as you'll soon see) that I realized that not once did any of the hummingbirds insert their bills into the corolla of the flower, where some part of the hummingbird's bill or head would come in contact with the stamens or pistils of the flowers, and thereby effect the pollination of this plant. Instead, the hummingbirds were "robbing" the nectar from the flowers by inserting their bills between the sepals and the petals, which lie flat against each other!

Perhaps this says something about my powers of observation, but I think it also illustrates the enlightening nature of observing hummingbirds and the flowers on which they feed.

What better reason is there for starting a hummingbird garden? Perhaps no reason is better than to try and discover the mysteries of hummingbird behavior, but to simply observe the combinations of hummingbird and flower colors together is certainly reason enough to have a garden especially designed to attract hummingbirds.

As Audubon says in his account of the Ruby-throated Hummingbird, "The prairies, the fields, the orchards and gardens, nay, the deepest shades of the forests, are all visited in their turn, and everywhere the little bird meets with pleasure and with food."

In the following chapters, we will explore just how, where, when, and why this is done, and how you can take part in this remarkable balance of nature's art and science.

2

Hummingbird Lives

~·~

Bartholomew's Cobble lies on the side of the Housatonic River in Berkshire County, Massachusetts. Once owned by Colonel John Ashley, a colonial statesman whose house still stands on the grounds, the Cobble served as a cow pasture in the 1800s for farmer George Bartholomew. Now a wildlife reserve and a National Natural Landmark, the Cobble contains 278 acres of wildflowers, tree seedlings, and perhaps the greatest number of naturally occurring fern species in the country.

It was here that I saw my first hummingbird nest in the wild (see Photo 2). Situated about fifteen feet high, on a lower limb of an eastern redcedar tree, the tiny, lichen-covered nest blended in perfectly with the peeling, lichen-covered branch on which it sat. I certainly would not have noticed it had I not been told of its exact location beforehand.

Michael Cuoco, Cobble naturalist, informed me that I was two weeks late, that all activity around the nest had ceased in the middle of June. Until then, he had seen the female Rubythroat sitting on the nest and making numerous trips back and forth to it. Although he hadn't actually seen her young, he assumed that she must have been incubating a couple of eggs up in that nest.

If the fledglings grew successfully, they would have been taking nectar from the wild columbine, which blooms in profusion at the Cobble from early to mid-May through June. The jewelweed and wild bergamot there bloom next, from the middle of July through August, and the cardinal flower provides nectar for the hummingbirds at the Cobble from August through September, when they prepare for their fall migration across the Gulf of Mexico and back to Central America.

As we can see, Bartholomew's Cobble provides everything that the Ruby-throated Hummingbird needs to survive and breed successfully— ample shelter for the nest, plenty of flowers loaded with nectar, and a pleasant climate.

But hummingbird lives are a lot more complicated and diverse than you might think, in spite of their diminutive size—or perhaps because of it. Understanding the keys to the hummingbird's physical makeup, energy requirements, and behavior patterns will go an exceptionally long way in helping you provide for these birds and make a home for them in your garden.

Because the hummingbird uses such an extraordinary amount of energy for its size, it requires an enormous amount of food relative to other animals, and at much more frequent intervals. Numerous studies have been done on just how much food a hummingbird eats and how many calories it expends in a day. I like Crawford Greenewalt's figures the best. According to Greenewalt, an average-sized man consumes 3,500 calories a day, but a similarly sized hummingbird would have to use 155,000 calories in that same time period in order to keep itself going. Put another way, that same man would have to eat 370 pounds of boiled potatoes each day in order to function like a hummingbird.

The conclusion to be drawn from figures such as these for hummingbird gardeners is obvious: It never hurts to have as many blossoms around for the hummingbirds as you can. By watching a male Anna's Hummingbird at the botanical gardens of the University of California at Berkeley, researcher Oliver Pearson discovered that the nectar from about 1,022 fuchsia blossoms would supply the energy needs of this hummingbird for a day. My own observations at the corner site of Chinese lantern bushes referred to earlier revealed that each plant contained about 200 flowers. There were four plants on the south-facing side of the corner, containing about 1,000 blossoms, and on the west-facing side, six more plants brought the grand total of Chinese lantern blossoms on that one corner site up to at least 2,500! And that doesn't include the flowers from all the other hummingbird plants in the immediate vicinity. No wonder there were usually two or three hummingbirds hanging around the Chinese lantern bushes every time I visited that corner site.

Once you get your hummingbird garden going, you will discover that hummingbirds undergo all of the usual functions of any other bird. They're just so small that you usually don't notice all of their intricate activities unless you are looking at them through a pair of binoculars or a telephoto lens or unless they're within a few feet of you.

For instance, after nectaring on a number of flowers for thirty seconds or so, a male hummingbird often returns to his favorite nearby perch, usually a bare, exposed branch that gives him a good view of the surrounding area (see Photo 3). (Females are generally more shy and secretive than males, and usually don't perch in such exposed areas.) Once back at his or her perch, the hummingbird might rub its bill back and forth against the branch in order to wipe off the residue of nectar, insects, pollen, and anything else with which its bill has come in contact during the foraging session (see Photo 5).

Then the hummingbird often engages in a meticulous preening session, in which it runs its primary flight feathers through its bill and picks at the feathers at the base of its wings and the body feathers on its chest. Then you might see it scratching its head with its foot, as a cat does.

Satisfied that all of its feathers are back in order, the hummingbird might enjoy a few moments of rest, though it is difficult to say for certain that any wild animal truly rests, even when it's asleep.

For instance, perching hummingbirds often turn their heads back and forth, seemingly for no reason at all other than to take in the scenery. But in addition to scanning the surrounding area for predators and interlopers that might compete for their supply of flowers, hummingbirds are extraordinary hunters of insects, often picking their prey right out of the air while they're hovering themselves.

I saw this happen once. One moment, the hummingbird was perched on the branch. Suddenly, a tiny speck appeared, moving across and below the hummingbird's line of vision. Instantly, the hummingbird dropped off its perch, just far enough to position itself alongside the fly and pick the insect out of the air with its bill. The hummingbird immediately returned to its perch a few feet above where the fly had been, and continued turning its head to the right and left, looking for other insects.

Indeed, in order to satisfy their protein requirements, hummingbirds supplement their nectar diet by consuming a wide variety of small insects and spiders, which they glean from flowers, grab from sap-covered tree trunks (they drink the sap, too), or catch in midair, as we have just seen.

Hummingbird gardener Marguerite Gross reports that the Monterey pines in her northern California yard provide good "gnatting" opportunities for hummingbirds (the pitch attracts and catches insects), while the hummingbirds in her garden also pick aphids off the lemon tree there, in addition to consuming the nectar from its flowers.

If you are observant, you may notice a hummingbird female building a nest in your yard—either in a nearby tree, in a potted plant, above a porch light, or somewhere else it discovers. Hummingbird nests may be found less than two feet off the ground or in the tops of trees over ninety feet high.

It usually takes the female from a few days to a week to build the nest, which she constructs from pieces of plant down and fibers, and holds together and fastens to the substrate with spider silk. Most hummingbird nests contain a soft lining of plant down and are camouflaged externally with bits of lichen or bark.

Hummingbird nests are extremely small (most average one to two inches in height and diameter), and therefore they are very difficult to spot. The best clue to finding one, according to Kimball Garrett, collections manager of the Section of Ornithology at the Natural History Museum of Los Angeles County, is observing a female going back and forth to a specific location. Follow the female, and you'll find the nest.

Female hummingbirds usually lay two eggs, a couple of days after mating and about forty-eight hours apart. The eggs are white, oval, and about the size of a bean. After the female incubates the eggs for a couple of weeks or so, the first egg hatches, normally followed a day or so later by the second. The tiny hummingbird that emerges from one of these eggs is usually about one centimeter in length, but it grows rapidly over the next few weeks as the female regurgitates protein-rich insects and nectar into the nestling's throat. Usually, the nestling is ready to fly from the nest by this time, but the female will continue to feed it for a couple more weeks, even when the fledgling has left the nest. After that, it's on its own and must fend for itself.

The range of hummingbird behavior is really quite extraordinary, and you should have a chance to see most of it in your garden. Take, for instance, the variety of male hummingbird mating displays, which also serve at times to frighten off intruders. I've seen them used for both purposes.

In the case of the former, it was in a canyon just north of Malibu, California. Embarking along the main trail, I soon heard a familiar sound—the high-pitched, squeaky, metallic "whzz-whzz-whzz" song of the male Anna's Hummingbird, the only hummingbird commonly acknowledged to have any type of a song at all.

Following the hummingbird's call, I took a side trail to the west about fifty yards and found myself in a grove of California sycamore trees. Knowing that the hummingbirds here would only be perching or nesting in the sycamore trees, I looked around for the nectar source that was supporting these hummingbirds (for where there's one hummingbird, there must be others).

Looking up, I found it—a long row of yellow-flowering tree tobacco running along the entire length of the west side of this field. A female Anna's soon made her presence known with her "chip-chip-chip" call, and she flew over from her perch (nest?) high in a sycamore tree to nectar from the tree tobacco flowers. After feeding for a minute or so, she took up a perch on an adjacent bush.

That's when the male went into action. First, he hovered about forty feet directly above the female, chipping several times. Then he slowly flew straight up to a height of about one hundred feet, held this spot for a moment, and then drifted off to the side and back down to the forty-foot mark. Then he dove down suddenly toward the female like a shot, dive-bombing at a forty-five-degree angle at about sixty miles an hour to within inches of her head, and emitting a high-pitched, squeaky "pop" as he went by the spot where she was perched. Immediately, he was back at the original hovering spot, chipping, rising up to the peak at about one hundred feet, and so on. He repeated this process four or five times, and then flew off to the south, no doubt to nectar or to rest after all of this frenetic activity.

Just four houses down the street from where I live, I saw a male Anna's use this very same display to chase off a much larger bird from one of its favorite perches in the front yard of a large home.

Indeed, hummingbirds (especially the males) can be quite pugnacious and intimidating to other birds no matter how large, in defense of their territory. At one tree in my neighborhood, I have seen a single Anna's male chase away a pair of house finches, a pair of yellow-rumped warblers, and even a group of six starlings almost three times its size.

As Marguerite Gross points out in a delightful article on the subject in *Bird Watcher's Digest,* hummingbird mating and territorial displays vary widely from species to species. While the Allen's male zips back and forth in a wide, shallow arc above the female before climbing to about a one hundred foot height and diving down at her with feathers whirring, the Black-chinned male limits its mating display to a series of swoops in a wide, shallow arc above the female (as does the closely related Ruby-throated Hummingbird). The Rufous Hummingbird describes an oval in the air, climbing slowly and diving quickly, while the Calliope hovers high at each side of a very wide, U-shaped arc.

The hummingbird's remarkable ability to fly results from the bird's anatomy and technique. In the first place, the hummingbird's wing is joined at the shoulder in such a way that it can be turned 180 degrees up or down; this enables the bird to gain upward draft on both the forward and backward strokes while hovering, simply by flipping its wings back and forth in a figure-eight pattern.

In addition, the hummingbird's wing muscles, which make up twenty-five to thirty percent of its total weight, enable the bird to obtain just as much power from the upward movement of the wings as from the downward flaps. Most birds have a relatively weak upstroke compared with the downstroke.

Therefore, when the hummingbird takes off from its perch, it is already moving at full speed, which in the case of the Ruby-throated Hummingbird is normally about twenty-five to thirty miles per hour around the garden, with its wings flapping about fifty times a second if it's a female and about seventy times a second if it's a male. However, when a male hummingbird goes into his courtship flight, his wings are often beating two hundred times per second, and his speed may reach in excess of sixty miles an hour.

But despite all of the hummingbird's truly extraordinary attributes, perhaps nothing has captured the imagination of hummingbird watchers throughout time as much as the bright, iridescent colors that are produced by the hummingbird's feathers.

Catesby, writing of the Ruby-throated Hummingbird, states, "The whole throat [is] adorned with feathers placed like the scales of fish, of a crimson, metallic resplendency," and Audubon, commenting on the same species, writes, "Its gorgeous throat in beauty and brilliancy baffles all competition."

Audubon's friend Thomas Nuttall, writing to the great naturalist about the Rufous Hummingbird, states that "it seemed like a breathing gem, or magic carbuncle of glowing fire, stretching out its gorgeous ruff, as if to emulate the sun itself in splendour." Another great naturalist, Arthur Cleveland Bent, describes this same species in the following fashion: "The brilliant scarlet of the rufous hummer's gorget [iridescent throat feathers], which often glows like burnished gold, puts it in the front rank as a gleaming gem, a feathered ball of fire."

Whether you are watching the Ruby-throated, Rufous, Allen's, Costa's, Anna's, or any other hummingbird for that matter, it is often difficult to think of the right words to use in order to describe the sudden, brilliant, shining onslaught of metallic colors you see.

I tend to rate my observations in the field on a kind of instinctive "wow" scale; the more times I find myself compulsively uttering "wow" as I watch something amazing, the more esteemed an animal's or a flower's physical attributes or behavior becomes in my eyes.

I have never found myself uttering the word "wow" more often than when I'm suddenly confronted with a brilliant flash of shining, metallic scarlet or purple coming from the throat or crown of an Anna's or a Costa's Hummingbird, hit by full sunlight when the sun is behind me.

The same is true of the bright, shining, light-green, scaly backs that most North American hummingbirds display when caught by the full rays of the sun (see Photo 6).

The brightness of these colors is due to the way they are formed. Unlike colors that are caused by pigments (which simply absorb some colors and reflect others), a hummingbird's iridescent blues, greens, reds, and purples are formed by the refraction of light through platelets that are contained in the barbules of each feather barb located on the outer third of certain feathers.

The effect is like that of a mirror reflecting back light, and the results are stunning—as Alexander Skutch says, "like a sunbeam suddenly breaking through a dark cloud."

If you become a successful hummingbird gardener, with just one plant or with many, with just one hummingbird or with a whole family or colony, you will no doubt spend many hours watching the entertaining and enlightening activities of these tiny birds as they go about the business of their daily lives.

But hummingbird lives, as well as the life cycles of the flowers on which they feed, occur on an annual and a perennial basis as well, and in the following chapter, we will explore the secrets behind the regions and seasons of hummingbirds and their favorite flowers.

3

Regions and Seasons

T he Arizona blue-throated hummingbird will always be associated in my mind with Ramsay [sic] Canyon, that interesting
bird paradise on the eastern slope of the Huachuca Mountains
in southeastern Arizona."

So writes Arthur Cleveland Bent in his book *Life Histories of North
American Cuckoos, Goatsuckers, Hummingbirds, and Their Allies,* published in
1940 by the United States National Museum, and probably containing
the last word on North American hummingbirds for its time.

Bent took a trip to Ramsey Canyon in 1922 with his friend and
fellow hummingbird researcher Frank C. Willard. The two stayed at
"Berner's place," where, as Bent reports, "a number of neat cottages and
small gardens are maintained for the summer colony. Here the stream
ran almost under our cabin; and here we often heard the loud buzzing of
the blue-throated hummingbird or observed its direct and rapid flight, as
it whizzed by our doorway along the stream. It seemed never to wander
far from the narrow confines of this mountain gorge and always seemed
to feel perfectly at home and unafraid among the cottages and gardens."

You can still see the Blue-throated Hummingbird in southeastern
Arizona, a region generally referred to as "hummingbird heaven." Two
other southeastern Arizona favorites, the Magnificent and Broad-billed

hummingbirds, overlap in much of the Blue-throated's range, which also includes southern New Mexico and western Texas.

As stated earlier, the Ruby-throated Hummingbird is the only hummingbird that occupies the eastern region of the United States. Of the remaining hummingbird species that breed in the United States, just about all of them can be seen at one time or another in southeastern Arizona and the surrounding areas.

Hummingbird expert Sally Spofford has recorded most of the hummingbird species that breed regularly north of Mexico, at the hummingbird feeders at her home in southeastern Arizona. She attracts eight of these species to her yard each year: the Blue-throated, Magnificent, and Lucifer, as well as the more widespread Black-chinned, Anna's, Broad-tailed, Rufous, and Calliope hummingbirds.

"Others we may see most years, but not every year," she states. These include the Violet-crowned, Broad-billed, and White-eared hummingbirds of southeastern Arizona, as well as the farther-ranging Costa's Hummingbird.

Indeed, throughout the West, the ranges of a number of hummingbirds combine to cover an extremely wide area and a diverse selection of habitats.

The Allen's Hummingbird, for instance, sticks to the California coast, while the Rufous Hummingbird migrates across most of western North America to as far north as southern Alaska, covering over two thousand miles each way. (The Ruby-throated Hummingbird is the only other North American species that migrates as far as the Rufous, but the Rubythroat adds an extra feat to the process by crossing the Gulf of Mexico, without stopping, on each leg of its journey from its Central American wintering grounds.)

The Broad-tailed Hummingbird is essentially a Rocky Mountain inhabitant, while the Black-chinned Hummingbird makes itself at home throughout most of western North America. Southwestern deserts constitute the range of the Costa's Hummingbird, while the Calliope Hummingbird may be seen throughout most of the West, although it breeds (as does the Rufous) primarily in the Northwest region.

The Anna's Hummingbird, the only resident hummingbird in North America (except for a Channel Islands subspecies of the Allen's Hummingbird), ranges primarily along the West Coast, from the Pacific Northwest to Baja California. In recent years, however, it has been increasing its range into Arizona, largely because of the planting of suburban gardens, to which it is supremely well adapted.

But because most North American hummingbirds migrate north from their wintering grounds in Mexico and Central America each spring and return back to these areas in the fall, they are only visible to hummingbird watchers in the United States at particular times of the year. Some exceptions to this rule are the Anna's, Allen's, and Costa's hummingbirds, which maintain winter populations in some parts of their North American ranges.

The Ruby-throated Hummingbird, for example, spends the months of December, January, and February in southern Mexico and Central America (although some birds spend the winter in southern Florida), but by the beginning of March, it has returned to mid-Florida and most of the Gulf Coast states.

Following the warmer temperatures and a succession of spring-blooming wildflowers, the Rubythroat reaches northern Georgia by the beginning of April and New York by the beginning of May. Following the late-blooming wildflowers and the warmer temperatures again, it starts south in September, reaching northern Georgia in October, mid-Florida in November, and Central America by December.

At the Edith G. Read Natural Park and Wildlife Sanctuary in Rye, New York, the Ruby-throated Hummingbird is usually seen in May and September, on its way to and from the more attractive breeding grounds to the north of the New York metropolitan area and its surrounding suburbs.

Ken Soltesz, park curator, tells an interesting story about a migrating swarm of twenty to thirty Ruby-throated Hummingbirds that suddenly arrived at the park one September afternoon and began feeding in a field of late-blooming jewelweed there, by the side of Long Island Sound.

This brief and unusual encounter (hummingbirds don't migrate in flocks) inspired Soltesz to start a hummingbird garden at the sanctuary that includes trumpet creeper, bee balm, and cardinal flower, as well as a number of hummingbird feeders.

By making the sanctuary more attractive to the migrating hummingbirds, Soltesz hopes that they will remain long enough to nest there in future years instead of just stopping by briefly and then moving on.

In planning your hummingbird garden, therefore, you may expect

to see hummingbirds that are migrating through your area, hummingbirds that are breeding in your area for a specific period of time
each year, or hummingbirds that remain in your area year-round. In
addition, some southern areas play host to wintering hummingbirds that
usually fly north to breed when the weather gets warmer.

In the case of the Anna's Hummingbird, however, colder temperatures have not deterred this hardy species (which is sometimes referred to as the starling of hummingbirds) from establishing itself in
recent years as a year-round resident in numerous populated areas of the
Pacific Northwest—aided in no small part by the proliferation of hummingbird feeders and plantings throughout this region.

Hummingbird researcher David Hutchinson, of the Seattle Audubon Society, reports that although the Rufous, Calliope, and Black-
chinned hummingbirds are programmed to migrate south from Washington State in the fall, no matter what, the Anna's Hummingbird now
often stays in Seattle and obtains nectar throughout the winter from
hummingbird feeders that people have left up, and from a succession of
fall- and winter-blooming garden flowers, including scarlet runner bean,
nicotiana, snapdragon, nasturtium, camellia, azalea, jasmine, Japanese
aralia, and fuchsia. It also feeds on various insects throughout the winter.

In addition to the hummingbirds themselves, the flowers, vines,
shrubs, and trees on which they feed have their own regions and seasons
as well.

Robert Leslie James, writing in *Castanea,* the journal of the Southern Appalachian Botanical Club, in September 1948, includes a compen-
dium of correspondences on this subject, and concludes, "I feel justified
by the information obtained from books, papers, letters and personal
observation to announce that the BIG EIGHT native hummingbird flowers east of the Mississippi are: Aquilegia canadensis [wild columbine],
Aesculus pavia [red buckeye], Impatiens biflora [jewelweed], Monarda
didyma [bee balm], Macranthera Leconti [now called *Macranthera flammea;* no common name], Bignonia (Tecoma, Campsis) radicans [trumpet
creeper], Lonicera sempervirens [trumpet honeysuckle], Lobelia cardinalis [cardinal flower]."

James adds: "The introduced hummingbird flowers receiving the
most mention in the books, papers and letters that I have seen include:
delphinium, scarlet sage, nasturtium, gladiolus, phlox, Japanese hon-

eysuckle, canna, tiger lily, petunia, hollyhock, mimosa tree, lilac . . . and weigela."

In 1955, C. Russell Mason, writing in *The Bulletin of the Massachusetts Audubon Society,* featured a diagram of a hummingbird garden at the Society's Cook's Canyon Wildlife Sanctuary, in Barre, Massachusetts, in which many of the flowers on James's list were included (Japanese honeysuckle, trumpet creeper, delphinium, bee balm, phlox, petunia, hollyhock, jewelweed), along with others such as spider flower, great Solomon's seal, and coral bells.

Today, if you visit the Massachusetts Audubon Society's Pleasant Valley Wildlife Sanctuary in Lenox, Massachusetts, you can see spider flower, great Solomon's seal, and coral bells attracting the hummingbirds there, as well as lilac, bee balm, delphinium, penstemon, lungwort, hosta, jewelweed, wild columbine, and ground ivy, among other popular hummingbird flowers.

Meanwhile, if you travel to the Arizona-Sonora Desert Museum in Tucson and look at the hummingbird garden there, you will find only a few of the hummingbird plants that are popular in the Northeast (small red morning glory, cardinal flower, and coral bells are about it), while there are plenty of hummingbird plants that are popular in the Southwest. These include ocotillo, chuparosa, golden-beard and Parry's penstemon, skyrocket, bladderpod, and bird of paradise.

According to Angelika Brinkmann-Busi of the California Native Plant Society, hummingbird plants for California include, in addition to ocotillo, chuparosa, and agave, various species of columbine, paintbrush, monkeyflower, penstemon, and sage. She also recommends woolly blue curls, California fuchsia, scarlet delphinium, and fuchsia-flowering gooseberry for California hummingbird gardeners.

Hummingbird expert Nancy Newfield, of the Orleans Audubon Society, recommends a number of plants for hummingbird gardeners in New Orleans that I have also found very popular in my neighborhood in Los Angeles. These include Chinese lantern, bottlebrush, and shrimp plant.

Some other flowers that Southeastern hummingbird gardeners might want to try include fire pink, red buckeye, and Texas mallow, while in the Northwest, fuchsia-flowering gooseberry is as popular for the hummingbirds there as it is in California. Northwestern hummingbird gardeners might also want to try red-flowering currant, madrone, orange honeysuckle, and great hedge nettle to attract hummingbirds in that region.

Just as hummingbird plants occupy different regions throughout North America, they have their own set of seasons as well. Indeed, hummingbirds rely on a succession of blossoming flowers throughout the year in order to sustain themselves and their young from the early-spring arrival of the adults to southern North America, through their travels to northern latitudes, throughout the breeding and nesting season, and along their southward migration in the fall, back to their overwintering grounds in Mexico and Central America.

In early spring, for instance, the blossoms of red buckeye, wild columbine, red-flowering currant, and ocotillo support hummingbirds in various parts of North America.

In late spring and early summer, more and more flowers come into bloom in order to sustain the increasing numbers of hummingbirds and their subsequent demand on the nectar supply of the flowers in each area. Summer-blossoming flowers such as beauty bush, coral bells, weigela, and scarlet sage can go a long way toward feeding these hummingbirds, while in late summer and early fall, the flowers of bee balm, cardinal flower, butterfly bush, and jewelweed can serve the same purpose.

As fall progresses, and even throughout the winter in some southern areas, the flowers of bottlebrush, California fuchsia, lantana, and Cape honeysuckle can supply nectar for hummingbirds that are still on the wing in these regions.

Furthermore, depending on the latitude and altitude of your garden, blooming times will vary. As hummingbird researcher Daniel F. Austin reports, for instance, the small red morning glory comes into bloom in southern Florida in May, but it doesn't bloom in the Northeast until July; and while the trumpet honeysuckle and trumpet creeper both come into bloom in southern Florida in March, they don't bloom in the Northeast until May and July, respectively.

It can be seen, therefore, that the more familiar you become with the regions and seasons of the North American hummingbird species that visit or reside permanently in your area, and the more familiar you become with the regions and seasons of the many types of flowers on which they feed, the better your chances will become to provide the food these hummingbirds need throughout the year, and by so doing, to provide yourself with the pleasure and entertainment of watching them in your yard for as long throughout the year as possible.

Perhaps someday you will be able to experience, in your hummingbird garden, what Percy Algernon Taverner and Bradshaw Hall Swales saw while observing the migrating Rubythroats for the first three days of September in 1906, on Point Pelee, Ontario, Canada, among the patches of jewelweed there:

"It [the jewelweed] was simply spangled with blossoms," they recall, "and all about and over it hovered and darted hundreds of Hummingbirds. From some little distance . . . we were aware of innumerable little twitterings that followed each other so rapidly as to scarce be separable, one from another. . . . Underlying this was a low hum that arose from the vibrations of many little wings."

If your hummingbird garden is located along the pathway of migrating Rubythroats, you may be able to attract a group of them to your garden, and then you'll be able to hear the little twitterings and the humming of many little wings in your own yard, just as Taverner and Swales did on Point Pelee. (The same can be said about migrating Rufous, Calliope, and Allen's hummingbirds, among others.)

But whether you are attracting Rubythroats in Boston, Anna's Hummingbirds in Los Angeles, Broad-tailed Hummingbirds in Denver, or Costa's Hummingbirds in Tucson, you'll want to provide as natural an environment as possible for them, including everything they need for their survival.

In the next chapter, we'll discuss the first steps you'll need to take in order to do just that.

4

Getting
Started

~·~

I n 1937, a man named Frank Bené moved to Phoenix, Arizona, for
reasons of health, and it was there, over the next few years, that he
developed an interest in ornithology that resulted in a work that
can only be described as a truly remarkable piece of amateur
naturalism.

In his book *The Feeding and Related Behavior of Hummingbirds with
Special Reference to the Black-chin,* published as Volume 9, Number 3, of the
Memoirs of the Boston Society of Natural History, Bené describes, with
the aid of charming accompanying diagrams, two hummingbird gardens
that he maintained at two separate residences that he had in Phoenix
from 1939 until 1941.

It would do a prospective hummingbird gardener well to make a
note of what Bené provided for the Black-chinned and Rufous hummingbirds that visited his yard during these years, for Mr. Bené gave
these hummingbirds everything they needed in order to consume an
adequate amount of nectar and insects, perch when necessary, roost at
night, occupy a nest, and raise their young.

Nectar came in the form of such flowers as lantana, aloe, nasturtium, and honeysuckle at the first house, and shrimp plant, canna, columbine, hollyhock, and bird of paradise at the second house.

Perching sites included ash trees, grapevines, clotheslines, and even electric wires, while oleander bushes provided the most desirable nesting sites for the females. Meanwhile, citrus and eucalyptus trees provided both perching and nectaring opportunities for the hummingbirds.

By providing a combination of shrubs, vines, and trees surrounding the garden, along with a good variety of hummingbird flowers and feeders (in the form of small bottles and open glasses) within the refuge that he had created, Bené was successful not only at attracting the hummingbirds to his yard initially but also at getting them to come back from one year to the next.

In 1940, for instance, at the first house, he recalls the arrival on March 19 of what he could only presume was one of the same female Blackchins that had nested in his yard the previous year.

"Immediately I stole to the rear yard to see if she had discovered the feeder," he writes, "but no sooner had I opened the kitchen screen door than she flew over to me from the clothesline, as though to greet me. For a moment I thought she would enter the kitchen. Then she returned to the clothesline. I picked up the feeder at the side of the house and walked up to her, but before I got to the clothesline she was in front of me, drinking from the feeder in my hand."

You, too, can achieve the familiarity that Frank Bené had with the hummingbirds in his garden, simply by following a few of the first steps in planning a hummingbird garden.

To start off, it is a good idea to become familiar with the plants that are the most successful at attracting hummingbirds in your immediate area—even within a few blocks of where you live.

If you take a walk around your neighborhood, you may notice hummingbirds using certain flowers for food. By making a note of which flowers the hummingbirds favor the most, you'll have a good head start toward attracting them into your yard by using the very same plants.

In my neighborhood of Los Angeles, for instance, I quickly discovered, by doing just a few days of local fieldwork, that the flowers preferred most by the hummingbirds in my neighborhood are (not necessarily in this order) Chinese lantern, Cape honeysuckle, pink powder puff (see Photo 4), lantana, tree aloe (see Photo 7), bottlebrush, acacia, eucalyptus, citrus, and bird of paradise, among others.

Although such flowers as snapdragon, azalea, and nasturtium are known to be attractive to hummingbirds, I have never seen a hummingbird nectaring on any of these plants in my neighborhood.

This doesn't mean that the hummingbirds don't ever utilize these flowers, or wouldn't if there were nothing else available. It just means that they prefer the flowers on the first list when given a choice.

Indeed, the flower preferences of hummingbirds are very strong, and once they're established, the hummingbirds are very predictable regarding which flowers they'll choose when offered a variety.

This can be used to your advantage in your garden, of course, for hummingbirds are creatures of habit, and as creatures of habit, they settle in nicely, and for long periods of time (depending on the species and the time of year), into a routine of feeding, perching, and roosting for the night, all within an extremely small area, considering their ability to range far and wide.

The male Anna's Hummingbird down the street from me, for instance, appears every morning perched on an exposed upper branch of a young California sycamore tree in my neighbor's front yard. During the day, between nectaring sessions on his favorite flowers in the immediate vicinity, he shifts his perch from the sycamore tree to two or three other trees in the front yard—often emitting his "whzz-whzz-whzz" call as a way to tell everybody and everything (including me) that this is his territory.

I don't know where this hummingbird roosts for the night, but every morning as I walk by that house, there he is, either on that sycamore tree or on one of the other trees, proclaiming a good morning to all—and "Stay away, this is my territory and foraging ground."

There is a row of azalea bushes planted around the front of this corner house, and yet I have never seen the hummingbird use them for nectar, although it does visit a few tiny young Chinese lantern bushes inside the yard, as well as a couple of red-flowering eucalyptus trees, and a coral tree, when in bloom.

I haven't asked the people who live in this house, but I'll bet they have no idea that they have a hummingbird in their midst (although they may wonder who that strange man is who stops outside their yard every day and stares up at an empty tree).

From a distance, the hummingbird may appear to be just a leaf, but, just like the leaf, it is very much alive. In many ways, not the least of which is due to this hummingbird's charmingly pugnacious temperament, I feel that the yard is as much his as it is the property of the people who live in the house. And who knows—it may be.

As you can no doubt see from this anecdote, you can very easily have a hummingbird practically cemented to your yard, without your even trying to attract him to your yard in the first place.

Imagine, then, how well you can do when you *do* try.

Indeed, you may want to expand your horizons beyond the limits of your own immediate neighborhood. By taking a few field trips into your local nature areas, you can discover some great plants that the hummingbirds in your neighborhood are sure to find just as irresistible in your yard.

For example, on my trip to the canyon just north of Malibu, I discovered that tree tobacco is just as popular with hummingbirds in the wild as it is said to be with "garden" hummingbirds. After that field trip, I would certainly have no hesitation about suggesting that hummingbird gardeners plant some tree tobacco in their yards.

Likewise, after watching a group of Rufous or Allen's hummingbirds (females and immatures of the two are almost identical in the field) early one August, in a feeding frenzy on the scarlet penstemon that was still in bloom in the mountains north of Los Angeles (see Photo 10), I would not hesitate for a moment to suggest that hummingbird gardeners in the Los Angeles area try out this pretty, red, tubular flower, or perhaps one of the similar-looking penstemons in the area, such as scarlet bugler or Eaton's firecracker.

People in different parts of the country can use the same technique to compile their own list of indigenous hummingbird plants that will be just right for the hummingbirds in their area.

Another convenient way to discover which flowers the hummingbirds in your area like the most is to visit a local botanical garden and see what they have growing there.

The North Carolina Botanical Garden in Chapel Hill, for instance, has the following hummingbird plants growing on its premises: wild columbine, trumpet creeper, hibiscus, cardinal flower, bee balm, scarlet sage, fire pink, and jewelweed. The garden also cultivates other flowers that hummingbirds like, including eastern redbud, sweet autumn clematis, wild bleeding heart, foxglove, beardtongue, and turtlehead.

You can also expand your knowledge of the hummingbird and

flower scene in your area by visiting a native plant or regular garden nursery or two, by attending a meeting of your local Audubon Society chapter or other birdwatching group, and by visiting your local natural history museum and talking to the people there about which flowers in your town the hummingbirds like the best, and which hummingbird species you can expect to see at different times of the year.

I've always found that firsthand experience goes a long way in studying nature. Once you've seen a plant or an animal in the field, it's hard to forget that plant or animal; and when you talk to people about nature and get firsthand information from them, it's hard to forget that, too.

By asking around about the hummingbirds and flowers in your area, you might even make a few new friends as well.

But once you decide which flowers you want in your hummingbird garden, you have to decide where you're going to place them, and in what combinations of shape, size, color, and so on.

In the first place, it is comforting to note that you can have a very successful hummingbird garden with just one type of hummingbird plant, with ten, or with many more—as far as your interest and energy take you.

Take Robert S. Woods, for example, a California hummingbird gardener in the early part of this century. Woods used only orange trees, for the most part—and what results he got!

"A dozen years' experience in raising oranges and other subtropical fruit at Azusa, California, not far from the mouth of the San Gabriel Canyon, in Los Angeles County," he wrote in 1927, "have given the writer an opportunity to become more or less familiar with six of the Californian species of Hummingbirds, which gather in considerable numbers in and about the orange groves during the blooming season, which usually coincides with the spring migration of most of these species."

Woods goes on to state that he has seen all six of these hummingbirds (Black-chinned, Costa's, Anna's, Rufous, Allen's, and Calliope) on his property "within less than 30 days, and at times in the month of April all but Allen's Hummingbird appeared to be present together."

Indeed, Woods could not be blamed for failing to attract the other Californian hummingbird to his yard, the Broad-tailed Hummingbird, as this species prefers the higher elevations in the mountain ranges to the north of where Woods's lowland orange groves were located.

At the other end of this continuum is Karen Sullivan, a hummingbird gardener in northern California who grows over three hundred hummingbird plants in her yard, and often has over twenty Rufous, Allen's, and Anna's hummingbirds flying around her property at any one time.

After moving into a new home, Sullivan purchased some native California penstemons and monkeyflowers, and she soon discovered that these plants, and plenty of others as well, proved to be very attractive lures for a growing number of hummingbirds in her garden. One thing led to another, and pretty soon she had everything from California fuchsia to cardinal flower, bee balm, and pineapple sage growing in her yard, along with many other hummingbird plants as well.

Most hummingbird gardeners will probably have neither one nor three hundred special plants for the hummingbirds that come to their yard, but some number in between these two extremes.

The hummingbird garden at the Arizona-Sonora Desert Museum has over forty species of hummingbird plants, while the Cook's Canyon garden in Massachusetts had over twenty.

One hummingbird gardener I visited in southern California had about fifteen good hummingbird plants in her corner yard, including lantana, camellia, azalea, fuchsia, citrus trees, lily-of-the-Nile, hibiscus, weigela, eucalyptus, and cup-of-gold vine. She also had a small hummingbird feeder hanging outside of her kitchen window, and while I was at the house, a female Anna's Hummingbird visited the feeder for an early-morning drink; the bird no doubt returned to the yard after I left, to drink some more of the sugar water in the feeder and to sample some of the flowers as well.

Meanwhile, my neighbor, with the Chinese lantern bushes around the corner of his property and an acacia tree inside his fence, has a steady supply of hummingbird activity in his yard with just these two plants (and the help of his neighbors' flowers).

The key to attracting hummingbirds, it seems, lies in the quantity of the flowers you provide as much as it does in any variety of those flowers. Of course, you must make sure that there is a steady supply of blossoming flowers from one season to the next, and some hummingbirds do like certain flowers more than other hummingbirds like those same flowers, but in general, as long as you provide enough nectar to satisfy the hummingbirds' prodigious energy requirements, they'll be happy and they'll no doubt remain close at hand.

Therefore, it's a good idea, when planning your hummingbird garden, to plant large amounts of flowers for the hummingbirds to notice from a distance. Once they know where their most convenient and effective source of food (from flowers or feeders) is located, these intelligent birds will keep on coming back for more food, as long as they remain in your area and are not migrating through.

This brings us to the idea of designing your garden. In general, it's probably best to put trees and shrubs in the back of your flower bed, and place the smaller flowering plants in the front of the flower bed. This way, depending on which way the flower bed is facing, both you and the hummingbirds will have an adequate view of the available flowers in the garden.

If you already have a fence or a trellis in place in your yard, this is the perfect place to put a climbing vine like Cape honeysuckle or trumpet creeper, while a gazebo would be even more ideal for plants like these.

Imagine sitting in your gazebo, fully protected from the sun, and watching the hummingbirds arrive to nectar at eye level, just a few inches away, while you sit on a comfortable, padded bench!

As Margaret Bodine discovered at her hummingbird porch in Maine in 1928, hanging baskets with flowers such as impatiens, geraniums, or fuchsia in them can be extremely attractive and useful to hummingbirds, which like to nectar while hovering high enough to avoid predators (including cats), and which like to have a good, open view of their surrounding environment.

You can also use window boxes, filled with such flowers as scarlet sage, nasturtium, petunia, phlox, or a combination of different flowers, to provide a good source of nectar for the hummingbirds, and one that is easily visible from the interior of your house.

In addition, well-placed pots around your garden can house such plants as fuchsia, nicotiana, penstemon, and geranium for the hummingbirds to use.

Another thing that the hummingbirds should have in your garden

is water—preferably running or dripping water, which provides the natural sounds and movement of a running stream, and proves to be an
exceptional lure for the hummingbirds.

The hummingbirds not only drink the water, they bathe in it as
well. A café in my neighborhood with an outdoor patio has a long,
narrow, stone-bottomed pool with recirculating water that cascades
down a gradual slope with mini-waterfalls built in, and ends in a circular
fish pool. The stones are embedded in the concrete bottom a couple of
inches below the surface of the water, but because a brown film of algae
has built up on it, the pool bottom really looks like a natural stream.

I took to watching a male Anna's Hummingbird that had established this pool and the row of Indian laurel fig trees that form a canopy
over it as his territory. One day, I saw him descend to the surface of the
water and, still hovering, lower his abdomen onto the surface of the
water as his feet disappeared below. He held this position for a few
moments, wings beating rapidly while his body moved forward and back
slightly, as if he were bathing and cooling himself at the same time—
which is probably exactly what he was doing.

Hummingbird gardener Marguerite Gross informs me of the following: "During warm weather or just sunny days, many times our
Anna's or Allen's hummers will fly in and out of the spray from a hand-
held hose, and they often fly quite close. If you stay quietly in one place,
they will bathe in close proximity.

"Hummers seem to enjoy a sprinkler whose spray rises up into the
lower branches of an overhanging tree or bush," she goes on. "They will
then perch on one of the branches caught by the spray and bathe and
preen for some moments. Thus, in a garden setting, fine spray sprinklers
are advantageous for attracting hummers."

Inexpensive recirculating pools can be built by using a small pump.
One hummingbird gardener I visited simply positioned a dripping hose a
foot or so above a shallow pool that she had created by digging a ten-
foot-wide hole in her backyard. She had cemented the bottom of the
pool and had covered the cement with soil and small stones to make it
look natural to the hummingbirds. Blood-red trumpet vine and Cape
honeysuckle grew on a fence beside the pool, and azalea, bird of paradise,
nasturtium, geranium, and peach and lemon trees also provided nectar
sources for the hummingbirds in the backyard. Meanwhile, out front,
the hummingbirds could feed on chasmanthe, grevillea, acacia, various

cacti, rose of Sharon, and cup-of-gold vine, as well as a hummingbird feeder placed on a second-story porch.

It can be seen, therefore, that the easier you make it for the hummingbirds to survive, and indeed, to flourish in your yard, the better your chances will be to achieve this very result. By providing these birds with the food, water, and shelter that they need in order to obtain enough energy on a daily basis to keep themselves alive, and enough space on a seasonal basis to breed and rear their young, you will no doubt be able to enjoy many hours of watching these hummingbirds carrying out the various activities of their lives.

By providing for the hummingbirds in this fashion, you will enjoy the benefits and the pride of having created not just a way station for the hummingbirds to find a snack and then move on; you'll have created a living garden, a hummingbird ecosystem that will perpetuate itself and evolve from one year to the next.

The diagram on pages viii and ix should give you some ideas for designing your own hummingbird garden. As you can see, the borders of the yard contain various shrubs and vines that attract hummingbirds, while a few well-placed trees will not only provide the hummingbirds with nectar, but will offer the birds some good perching and nesting sites.

While this diagram features many hummingbird plants that are popular in my neighborhood of Los Angeles, most of these plants can easily be used in other parts of the country, or can be replaced by similar types of plants (i.e., trees, vines, shrubs, and wildflowers, as well as common garden flowers) that grow best or are the most easily available for gardeners in each specific region.

5

Hummingbird Flowers

A t the National Wildflower Research Center in Austin, Texas, there is a "pollinator garden" containing numerous plants that bees, moths, butterflies, and hummingbirds pollinate. The hummingbird plants include scarlet gilia, autumn and mountain sage, Bacchus's and Murray's penstemon, heartleaf hibiscus, and flame acanthus. The hummingbirds also share a few of the flowers of the other pollinators, including butterfly weed and lantana, which the butterflies use. But although hummingbirds are capable of pollinating some of the flowers that certain insects pollinate, there is a special type of flower that is pollinated primarily by hummingbirds.

Hummingbirds and the flowers they pollinate have coevolved over the millennia. In return for providing the hummingbirds with their much-needed nectar, the hummingbirds transfer pollen from one flower to the next by brushing their heads, bills, chins, and other body parts against the anthers and stigmas of the flowers, and thus enable these plants to reproduce.

According to researchers Karen and Verne Grant, it is more than likely that hummingbird flowers evolved in the tropics from those flowers that are pollinated primarily by bees, but also from some of the flowers that are pollinated by butterflies and moths.

Somewhere along the evolutionary line, longer-tubed flowers appeared; the hovering hummingbirds, with their long bills, could reach
inside them for their nectar, while most of their insect competitors could
not.

As the hummingbirds and the flowers they pollinated spread to the
north across North America, the intimate relationship between these
birds and their favorite flowers became established in many new areas,
from Maine to California and from Alaska to Florida.

As most students of hummingbird flowers are quick to learn, the
primary color of these flowers (at least in the wild) is red or some related
color, such as orange or pink. This is probably because red, as a comple-
mentary color to green on the color wheel, presents a strong contrast,
thus making the flowers stand out from the green foliage to the often-
migratory hummingbirds.

Furthermore, since bees do not see red, this excludes them from
competing with the hummingbirds for these flowers, and since these
flowers have no scent as a rule, they are largely ignored by bees, butterflies, and moths, which rely on scent to a great degree in locating their
nectar sources.

In addition, while bees and butterflies require that their flowers
have landing platforms on which to perch while nectaring, the flowers
that hummingbirds use for their nectaring needs are often pendent in
nature and have petals that are curved backward or downward or have
protruding stamens and stigmas that block the entrance to the flower
tube to virtually all visitors except the hovering hummingbirds, who can
poke their bills in from a distance.

All of this holds great significance for the hummingbird gardener,
because, since the floral needs of hummingbirds are so specialized, by
providing just the right flowers, you can be almost sure that if a hummingbird is in your area, it will come into your yard to utilize the flowers
that it needs in order to survive.

Although red is probably the most popular flower color among
hummingbirds, these birds visit flowers of a great many other colors for
nectar, including those with pink, orange, yellow, blue, purple, and
white flowers. Thus, a successful hummingbird garden could have a
number of red flowers, such as bee balm and Indian paintbrush, along
with a variety of flowers with other colors, such as the orange jewelweed
or Cape honeysuckle; the yellow tree tobacco or bladderpod; and a blue

penstemon or morning glory as well as the aptly named woolly blue curls.

One hummingbird garden in southeastern Arizona, for instance, contains the red golden-beard penstemon and Texas betony, the pink Lemmon's sage, and the beautiful, appropriately named golden columbine as a delightful accent. All of these flowers, along with a few other red ones such as California fuchsia and western coral bean, serve to attract fourteen species of hummingbirds, from the locally abundant Magnificent, Blue-throated, and Broad-billed hummingbirds to the more widespread Black-chinned, Anna's, and Calliope hummingbirds.

Meanwhile, at the Pleasant Valley Wildlife Sanctuary in Lenox, Massachusetts, Marilyn Flor, resident naturalist, reports that the Ruby-throated Hummingbird enjoys visits to the red bee balm, penstemon, and columbine there, as well as to the pink spider flower and coral bells, the blue delphinium and lungwort, the purple ground ivy, the lavender lilac and hosta, the white great Solomon's seal, and the orange jewelweed.

Of course, when it comes to choosing the flower colors of your own hummingbird garden, this is largely a matter of personal preference. The same is true of the ratio of cultivated flowers to wildflowers that you'll want to use.

While cultivated flowers such as Chinese lantern, lion's tail, and grevillea come from South America, Africa, and Australia respectively, they are extremely effective at attracting our North American hummingbirds to their blossoms, even though hummingbirds don't even exist on the latter two continents.

However, since hummingbirds have evolved so intricately with the native plants in each area of the United States, it seems only natural that hummingbird gardeners should incorporate at least some of these local wildflowers into their gardens as often as they can.

One day in early spring, while I was visiting the Theodore Payne Foundation, a native plant nursery in Sun Valley, California, I happened upon a male Costa's Hummingbird who had set up a perching and foraging area right outside the front door of the main building there. While visitors walked past him, many not even noticing that he was there, this hummingbird took nectar from a number of bladderpod plants (see Photos 8 and 9) as well as from the adjacent woolly blue curls (see Photo 11) and from a large western redbud tree.

Right there, in this desertlike microhabitat on the outskirts of the Los Angeles metropolitan area, were three excellent hummingbird plants that would grow easily in local gardens and would have the extra benefits of requiring less water than most cultivated flowers as well as adding a touch of native flora to someone's yard.

The principle of using local wildflowers in your hummingbird garden can be applied in any region of the country—for instance, with ocotillo and chuparosa in the Southwest, Texas mallow and coral bean in the Southeast, wild columbine and jewelweed in the Northeast, and firecracker flower and red-flowering currant in the Northwest.

In addition to using both wildflowers and cultivated plants, hummingbird gardeners can select from annual, perennial, and biennial flowers, depending on the requirements that they have for their gardens. Annuals such as nasturtium, petunia, and snapdragon, for instance, will provide many months of blossoming flowers for the hummingbirds (and color for the gardener), while perennials such as butterfly weed, bee balm, and columbine, and biennials such as hollyhock and foxglove, may have shorter flowering seasons (especially in colder areas), but provide the convenience of living from one year to the next, and often well beyond that.

Meanwhile, hummingbird plants such as impatiens, phlox, and geranium lend themselves well to growing in pots (whether hanging or on the ground), and therefore can be moved around the yard or the patio easily and can also be used in smaller areas, such as apartment balconies. Indeed, a good combination of hummingbird flowers in window boxes and hanging baskets, combined with a hummingbird feeder or two, can create a hummingbird garden in just about any apartment environment.

Flowerpots can also be used, in colder regions, for such plants as fuchsia, lantana, and nicotiana, in order to bring them indoors to protect them from freezing during the winter months.

In warmer areas of the country, bromeliads such as aechmea, tillandsia, and guzmania can be grown in pots (hanging or otherwise), and can also be attached to slabs of bark (or other substrates) and hung from various structures around the garden, such as the eaves of houses or the limbs of trees. One hummingbird gardener I visited had interspersed a number of tillandsia plants, which he had attached to pieces of cork bark, in various places amid a row of hummingbird feeders suspended from a latticework trellis overhanging his backyard patio. Thus, when the hummingbirds came up to visit the hummingbird feeders, they could also take a few sips from the tillandsia, as long as they were already in the area.

As hummingbird gardener Betty Davenport of the American Penstemon Society explains, different species of hummingbird plants from the same flower genus may have various shapes, colors, and blooming periods. Davenport has used many species of penstemon to attract hummingbirds to her gardens in the states of Washington, Arizona, and now California.

"There are penstemon species that are around four inches tall," she tells me, "and those that grow five feet tall. Flower colors include red, blue, white, yellow, pink, and purple, as well as bicolors. You will find penstemon shrubs, ground covers, border perennials, specimen plants, and rock-garden plants. By growing a number of penstemons, you can have bloom from early spring to July and August, and even longer in some cases.

"In Washington," she recalls, "hummingbirds came to my garden about twice a year and stayed about a week. They visited only the penstemons, although I had a number of lilies and columbines growing alongside the penstemons. After moving to Arizona, I purchased some penstemons and set the pots outside before I planted the flowers. Within minutes of setting the plants outside, the hummingbirds were fighting over them. When penstemons were in bloom, the hummingbirds visited them first, before going to my feeders. Hummingbirds will visit the blue flowers of penstemons, but they prefer the red and pink flowers."

As we can see, then, from following Betty Davenport's example, many different varieties of the same type of flower will be attractive to hummingbirds in your garden. However, it is important to note that cultivated hybrids of some hummingbird plants, such as penstemon and columbine, may be of little or no use to hummingbirds, as these flowers may have little or no nectar in them. Double varieties of cultivated flowers, such as fuchsias, may also be useless for hummingbirds, since they may find it difficult, if not impossible, to get their beaks and tongues into the flowers. In general, then, it is a good idea for hummingbird gardeners to utilize "species" plants in their gardens, whether these plants are native to the United States or are from some other part of the world.

It should also be noted here that hummingbirds often visit flowers, such as those of citrus trees and thistles, in order to gather up insects.

This is especially the case when females are feeding their young, as the nestlings require a large amount of protein at this stage in their lives, which the insects provide.

Hummingbirds are also attracted to the sap of trees, so if you have a sapsucker that has been poking holes in your apple or birch trees, don't be surprised to see a hummingbird or two flying up into the trees to feed from the sap flows, as well as on the insects that are attracted to the sap.

While you are observing the hummingbirds in your garden, you should have a good opportunity to see the interesting ways in which these birds pollinate the flowers on which they feed. For instance, one day in late March in Malibu, while watching a Rufous or Allen's hummingbird (females and immatures of the two are almost identical in the field) feeding from a Cape honeysuckle, I could see very clearly the flower's yellow-tipped anthers brushing the top of the hummingbird's head, which was buried so far into the flower tube that the hummingbird was only visible from its eyes back. Sure enough, when this hummingbird emerged from the flower and perched on a nearby branch a few moments later, I could see a large yellow patch of pollen on top of its head (see Photos 12 and 13). This same type of floral mechanism will cause blue pollen from the ethereally beautiful woolly blue curls to be brushed onto the top of the head of any hummingbird that takes nectar from this flower.

Meanwhile, with small flowers, such as those of lantana, the yellow pollen is picked up from one flower and deposited on the next by the hummingbird's bill, the tip of which is often speckled or even covered with this yellow pollen (see Photo 14).

As I mentioned earlier, the Anna's Hummingbirds in my neighborhood have learned to "rob" nectar from Chinese lantern flowers by sticking their bills between the petals from the side, instead of entering the flower from the front, where the anthers and stigmas are located.

Similarly, the hummingbirds in my neighborhood have discovered a way to rob the flowers of the blood-red trumpet vine of their nectar. It works like this: First, carpenter bees arrive and chew holes in the base of the flower tubes in order to rob the nectar themselves. Then the hummingbirds come by and dip their bills into the holes that the bees have made, thus robbing the flowers for a second time. Of course, if the bees have not been there first, the hummingbirds can still obtain nectar from the front end of these flowers, but this doesn't seem to be as desirable for them, because it means that they have to bury most of their body into the flower, thereby losing their view of the surrounding area, including any predators that may be nearby.

In most instances, however, hummingbirds will be drawn to your garden in order to obtain nectar, and thereby pollinate the flowers you provide, in the normal manner to which these birds have become accustomed throughout eons of evolution—as hummingbird observer Andrew Pickens described, in 1927, regarding the Ruby-throated Hummingbird and one of Robert James's "BIG EIGHT native hummingbird flowers east of the Mississippi": namely, *Macranthera flammea,* a tubular orange flower in the figwort family.

"I found one large patch of these brilliantly colored flowers in the edge of a small swamp," he writes, "and such twittering hordes of Ruby-throats I have seen about no other flower, not even excepting, what I had considered Hummingbird-beloved, buddleia. It was note-worthy that practically each bird had a yellow spot just above the nape."

What Pickens discovered was that the pistils of these upright flowers were longer than the stamens when the flowers came into bloom, and the pistils (and indeed the entire flower itself) would be pulled into a horizontal position, and thus onto the top of the hummingbird's head, while the bird was taking nectar from the flower. At this very moment, the pistil picked up pollen that had been deposited on this very same spot on the hummingbird's head by the stamens of another *Macranthera flammea* flower, which grow longer themselves a day or two after the flower comes into bloom, by which time the pistils have withered and dropped out of the way.

This floral mechanism ensures cross-pollination of this species of flower, and as Pickens reports, this results in "a riot of Hummingbirds" around the *Macranthera flammea* for days and weeks on end.

"Of all the forms that I have studied," he goes on, "this is the most exclusively Hummingbird flower, and I recall seeing no other honey-gatherers in its vicinity. I do not think it would be possible for a bee or a moth to effect cross-pollination, so elaborately is the whole scheme adapted to bird-pollination."

In Pickens's time, *Macranthera flammea* had no common name, and this is still the case with this flower, which occurs in the southeastern United States. Perhaps from now on we could call it Pickens's Hummingbird Flower.

Numerous observers of hummingbirds and the flowers that they utilize the most often have discovered that a large number of these flowers are in the figwort family (including paintbrush, penstemon, monkeyflower, and Mr. Pickens's *Macranthera*).

But as Frank Bené says regarding the diversity of floral designs in hummingbird flowers (outside of the tubular feature), "The most significant aspect of design is the fact that the hummingbird chooses no special design. Any design is suitable so long as it fits the hummer's feeding adaptation and makes access to the nectar possible.

"The predominating element of form of the hummingbird flower is the tubular feature," he goes on. "It makes no difference to the bird what part of the flower yields the tubular feature."

Indeed, as Bené indicates, hummingbird flowers, while sharing a number of the same basic attributes, occur in a wide variety of shapes and sizes, and come from a large number of plant families.

In addition to the figworts mentioned above, many hummingbird flowers are in the mint family (bee balm, sage, hedge nettle, and woolly blue curls), the mallow family (hibiscus, Texas mallow, and hollyhock), and the buttercup family (columbine and delphinium). Others come from the phlox family (skyrocket and phlox), the lily family (firecracker flower and red-hot poker), the saxifrage family (coral bells and red-flowering currant), the nightshade family (red cestrum and tree tobacco), the honeysuckle family (orange and trumpet honeysuckle), and the acanthus family (chuparosa, desert honeysuckle, and shrimp plant), to name just a few. And this list doesn't even include trees such as red buckeye, madrone, eucalyptus, and silktree!

In 1983, researchers Pat Murphy and John V. Dennis conducted a nationwide "hummingbird survey" in which they recorded 107 hummingbird flowers from across the United States. The most often mentioned were azalea, bee balm, canna, columbine, coral bells, fuchsia, geranium, honeysuckle, impatiens, petunia, rose of Sharon, sage, silktree, and trumpet creeper; the most popular of *these* flowers were fuchsia, honeysuckle, impatiens, petunia, and sage.

But despite the wide variety of flowers that are available to hummingbird gardeners across the country, the best way to ensure success in your own hummingbird garden is to use whatever flowers work the best for you, in your own area of the country, and especially in your own neighborhood.

Hummingbirds have very good memories, and they learn things very quickly, so when they discover a new flower on which to feed (especially one that is rich with nectar), they may soon prefer it over all others; and if they're a migratory species, they'll often remember it the following year, when they return to your garden.

So whether you use many, a few, or only one type of hummingbird plant in your hummingbird garden, the most important thing is that the hummingbirds like the flowers you're providing, and that you do as well.

In addition to providing flowers as a natural nectar source for hummingbirds, you can also provide a man-made source of nectar, one to which hummingbirds have become extremely well adapted over the years—namely, the hummingbird feeder.

This is the subject of our next chapter.

6

Hummingbird Feeders

In his book *Birds Over America,* Roger Tory Peterson describes a visit that he paid to a Mr. B. F. Tucker, "whose home in Modjeska Canyon, south of Los Angeles, has become a showplace."

According to Peterson, Mr. Tucker had built a "hummingbird cafeteria," which consisted of "a long rack of quart bottles filled with sugar water.

"Each jar," Peterson explains, "cleverly constructed so as to discourage ants and bees, could accommodate four hummingbirds simultaneously. Dozens of hummers buzzed about the flasks that lined the full length of the porch, and Tucker told me that several hundred made their headquarters in the canyon.

"To fully savor the jewel-like beauty of the feathered mites that hovered an arm's length away as he sat in his easy chair," Peterson goes on, "Tucker rigged up a fluorescent spotlight. A flip of a switch brought out the full iridescence—emerald, ruby, flame and amethyst—of each species as it came to sip the nectar."

Mr. Tucker's former home is now the Tucker Wildlife Sanctuary, and at various times of the year, you can see the Costa's, Black-chinned, Anna's, Rufous, Allen's, and maybe even the Calliope Hummingbird on this twelve-acre preserve.

But the key attraction at the sanctuary is the observation porch, a raised platform (on the site of the old house) with sliding glass doors (these are new), that looks out on a row of nine hummingbird feeders hanging from two long wires—five feeders on top and four below, staggered so that no one feeder is directly above another.

Since the porch is raised and the feeders are about an arm's length away from the sliding glass doors (so you have to watch your step!), you can get a close-up, eye-level view of the hummingbirds nectaring, without bothering them at all.

This same principle could be used by hummingbird gardeners throughout the country to great effect, if they happen to have a porch on the premises or want to build one.

As stated earlier, Margaret Bodine used small bottles filled with sugar water on her second-story porch in Maine to attract the hummingbirds there.

"These bottles are fastened among the blossoms and are speedily discovered by the Humming Birds," she writes. "Once found, there are few daylight hours from the middle of June till September when at least one is not there. Sometimes as many as eight are feasting at a time.

"On the day after our arrival at our summer home last year," she adds, "we put the little bottles out, and in less than ten minutes the first Hummer came, drank, and perched."

Perhaps the most original hummingbird feeder I've heard about is also one of the oldest ones that I've seen a reference to in the literature. The idea is Caroline G. Soule's, of Brookline, Massachusetts, and she wrote about her unique hummingbird feeder in the October 1900 issue of *Bird-Lore* magazine.

"One day I painted a trumpet-flower in water-colors," she writes, "on a rather stiff piece of Whatman paper. I painted it as a real flower would look if slit down on one side and spread flat, and I colored both sides. Then I cut out the flower, bent it into shape, and fastened the edges together. Inside the tube I put a small, cylindrical bottle, and tied the flower to the trumpet-creeper in an almost normal position. The little bottle I filled with sugar-and-water, not too thick.

"To my delight," she goes on, "the Hummingbird visited that flower with no more hesitation than the real ones, and very soon preferred it, and I had to fill up the bottle at least twice a day.

"One day I tried holding the flower in my hand, at a little distance from the creeper, and the hummingbird flew to it as fearlessly as if I were a vine."

Soule left her feeder-flower on the trumpet creeper until most of the flower's color was washed away by the rain, and then she took it down.

Seven years later, in National, Iowa, Althea Sherman and her sister E. Amelia, having read Caroline Soule's descriptions in *Bird-Lore,* began a series of experiments involving their own design for artificial flower-feeders—in this case, simulating nasturtium and tiger lily blossoms.

But the Shermans made their flowers more durable than Soule's by using white oilcloth, stiffening the edges with a strand of picture-cord wire, and painting them with oil colors instead of water colors. Just like Caroline Soule had done, they placed bottles of sugar water inside the artificial flowers.

After succeeding in getting the hummingbirds (Rubythroats) to visit their yellow nasturtium and red tiger lily flower-feeders, the Shermans were able to get the hummingbirds to visit a green-colored nasturtium flower-feeder, even though it was placed in the middle of green foliage.

Eventually, the Sherman sisters eliminated the artificial flower design altogether, as they added a bare bottle to their garden collection, wrapping it in unbleached muslin nailed to a stick.

The hummingbirds accepted the flowerless bottle, too, so the Shermans added two more similar bottles to the garden setup, and these were visited by the hummingbirds as well.

"One is led to wonder if the Homeric gods on high Olympus were more deeply stirred by the appearance among them of the youthful Ganymedes bearing cups of nectar, than are the Hummingbirds at sight of their cup-bearer," Sherman writes.

"Possibly not one of them is in sight when the door is passed," she adds, "yet instantly the air seems filled with them: some swinging back and forth in the air, squeaking and fighting, or darting from bottle to bottle thrusting in their bills as they pass, while an over-bold one will buzz about my head, sometimes coming under the porch in her zeal for the meeting."

During his hummingbird feeding experiments at his hummingbird gardens in Phoenix from 1939 to 1941, Frank Bené used a combination of small bottles and open glasses that were filled with sugar water and honey water.

Bené discovered that as soon as the hummingbirds tried the solution made with white sugar, "they unmistakably chose this in preference to other sweets." (The hummingbirds, of course, continued to use the flowers in his yards.)

Indeed, in recent years it has been shown that honey solutions are not only less tasty to hummingbirds than are white-sugar solutions (which most closely approximate the ingredients of flower nectar), but honey solutions can often be fatal to hummingbirds by causing a fungus infection in the hummingbird's tongue.

At the Tucker Wildlife Sanctuary, a solution of four parts water to one part white granulated sugar (the recommended ratio) is used in the hummingbird feeders in front of the observation porch as well as in those hanging from various trees around the sanctuary.

Some of the popular hummingbird feeders at the sanctuary feature a design that is commercially available. These feeders consist of a small bottle; a rubber stopper that fits snugly into the mouth of the bottle; a narrow, curved glass tube that is placed through a hole in the center of the rubber stopper; and a red plastic tip (with a small hole in the center of it) that covers the end of the glass tube. The hummingbirds feed on the nectar through the tiny hole in the center of the red plastic tip.

Of course, many different types of hummingbird feeders are commercially available in various shapes and sizes. Some are shaped like a flying saucer, while others are tall and cylindrical; some have landing platforms for the hummingbirds, while others do not.

But whichever type of hummingbird feeder you decide to use, or how many, there are a number of guidelines that you can follow to make sure that both you and the hummingbirds are well served by the feeders you provide.

In the first place, hummingbird feeders should be easy to clean and should not contain unreachable nooks and crannies where algae, mold, and bacteria can build up. Hummingbird feeders need to be cleaned and refilled at least once each week (and at least every few days in hot weather and when feeders are situated in direct sunlight) in order to keep the sugar water from spoiling and to keep mold, which can be harmful or fatal to hummingbirds, from forming.

As stated earlier, artificial nectar for hummingbird feeders should consist of a four-to-one solution of water and white granulated sugar. This solution should be boiled for a couple of minutes in order to dissolve the sugar completely, retard fermentation of the mixture, and destroy microorganisms, such as mold and bacteria, that are in the water. If you add some extra water to the solution before you boil it, you can be sure that the mixture is no stronger than four-to-one after boiling. Otherwise, you could harm the hummingbirds. (A five-to-one solution is also acceptable.) Excess solution can be stored safely in the refrigerator for about a week.

Honey should not be used in any nectar solution, nor should brown sugar or artificial sweeteners, as all of these items can be harmful to hummingbirds. In addition, red food coloring does not need to be added to any nectar solution, as it is unnecessary for attracting hummingbirds to feeders. Buying commercially prepared nectar solutions is also unnecessary, as these solutions often contain ingredients that are not present in the hummingbird's natural diet and that hummingbirds don't need.

Hummingbirds will be attracted to the red color that is featured on most hummingbird feeders, and once they discover where a hummingbird feeder is, they don't need to be reminded of its whereabouts. Indeed, as many hummingbird gardeners have discovered, these intelligent birds will even remember where a feeder was located the previous year, and will hover around that area when they return, even if the feeder is no longer at that exact spot.

Althea Sherman states that on June 6 of the fifth season of her hummingbird-feeding experiments, a returning hummingbird "flew to the spot always occupied by the flower-pot holding the artificial flowers, when they were in place. Over this vacant spot she hovered an instant before flying away.

"In the sixth spring," Sherman goes on, "the species arrived earlier than usual. No bottles were out on May 7 when a Hummingbird was seen hovering over the customary place for the artificial flowers. As quickly as possible these flowers were put out, but before they could be filled the bird was thrusting her bill into the tiger-lily."

Observations such as these led the Sherman sisters to conclude "that the same birds were returning to us summer after summer."

Indeed, the following year, Althea Sherman found herself "in the orchard a hundred feet or more distant from the bottles, when a Hummingbird flew toward me and buzzed about my head as do no other birds except those that are fed. With greatly accelerated pulse I hurried to the house and filled the bottles. In exactly two minutes the Hummingbird was drinking from one of them; this was the first drinking witnessed in that year. It was one of my most thrilling experiences in bird study. Two marvelously long journeys of from one to two thousand miles each had this small sprite taken since last she had drunk from the bottles, yet she had not forgotten them, nor the one that fed her."

In addition to the guidelines for hummingbird feeder use that we've just discussed, some other pointers include the following: make sure that the feeder is placed in the shade (or at least partial shade), so the nectar solution won't ferment as quickly as it would if the feeder were situated in direct sunlight; separate your feeders by at least six feet, or even place them out of sight of each other, so that one hummingbird can't dominate all of your feeders; and provide for the control of insect visitors such as ants, bees, and wasps.

In order to keep ants away from your hummingbird feeders, you might want to use an "ant moat," which consists of a small cup filled with water that attaches to the wire above the feeder. When the ants climb down a wire in the center of the cup, and discover the water, they turn around and go back up the wire. A number of ant moats are available commercially, and some hummingbird gardeners make their own as well.

In order to keep flying insects such as bees away from the hummingbirds' nectar, you can periodically clean away any spillage around the feeder's openings with a water-dampened cloth or paper towel. One hummingbird gardener I visited simply filled her hummingbird feeder to a little bit lower than the recommended level, and she found that while the hummingbirds could still reach the nectar, the bees couldn't.

It is well-known among hummingbird gardeners that an aggressive male can dominate a feeding area and prevent the use of any feeders in this area by juvenile hummingbirds and adult females as well as by other adult males. Females can be extremely selfish when it comes to feeders, too, especially when they're building their nests in preparation for raising their young.

However, by placing your hummingbird feeders at least six feet away from each other, you will make it extremely difficult for any one hummingbird to dominate all of the feeders at the same time. Many hummingbird gardeners place feeders out of sight of each other, so that while a hummingbird is using one feeder, it is unaware of any competing activity at the other ones.

Frank Bené used this arrangement at his hummingbird garden in Phoenix in 1940, when two female Blackchins were competing for his feeders; the more aggressive female was even successful at driving away any male Blackchins that visited the yard.

So Bené "placed one feeder at the rear of the house, one at the side between the house and the row of oleander, and a third in the front. The object of this arrangement was to conceal the . . . feeders so that a bird feeding from one would not be seen by another feeding from a second feeder.

"For a while the trick worked," Bené recalls. "But [the pugnacious female] was smarter than I expected her to be. Instead of confining her observation post to the ash twig in front of the house, she added a third post, the twig of a eucalyptus, from which station she could view both the rear and side of the house. By shifting from perch to perch she commanded a clear view of all the feeders."

Frank Bené isn't the only person ever to be outsmarted by a hummingbird. One day, while I was visiting a hummingbird gardener in Montpelier, Vermont, I played a cat-and-mouse game with a male Rubythroat that had established the yard as his territory and was using two feeders positioned along one side of the house—one near the front and one near the back.

As I tried to take a photograph of him at one of the feeders by positioning myself in advance, this hummingbird invariably ended up at the other feeder, about thirty feet away. After about fifteen minutes of running from one feeder to the other, I finally figured out how he knew where I was all of the time.

The hummingbird had two perches: one on top of an antenna at the front of the house and another on top of an antenna at the rear of the house. From these two observation posts, he could survey the activity at each of the feeders, and by so doing, he could take the appropriate action, depending on what was happening at each of them.

During April and September in southeastern Arizona (hummingbird migration season), Sally Spofford often has forty to fifty hummingbirds that visit at least twenty feeders in her yard, consuming about two gallons of sugar water each day.

But whether you have a big operation like Sally Spofford's, or just one feeder outside your kitchen window, you should always keep at least some nectar in the feeder for the hummingbirds, even if you go away on vacation. (You can always get someone to take care of the feeder while you're gone.) After all, it's unfair to the birds to let your feeder run dry, and sometimes it can even be hazardous—for instance, if the hummingbirds come to rely on your feeder, and a cold snap hits.

In colder areas, you should have your hummingbird feeders in place before the hummingbirds start arriving in the spring, and you can leave the feeders up until the hummingbirds have left in the fall. Migrating species of hummingbirds will head south in the fall, even if there are flowering plants and nectar-brimming feeders available to them.

In regions where hummingbirds occur on a year-round basis, hummingbird feeders can be maintained throughout the year. Even in the Pacific Northwest, as David Hutchinson reports, hummingbird feeders (as well as winter-flowering plants and other food sources, such as tree sap and insects) help to maintain the resident population of Anna's Hummingbirds during the winter.

According to Hutchinson, hummingbird gardeners in Seattle use numerous techniques to keep their hummingbird feeders operating properly during these colder times of the year. Some people have a number of feeders ready, so when the nectar in one freezes, it's brought inside while a new one is placed outside. Hummingbird feeders can also be wrapped in socks or a warm fabric, and the hummingbirds will still visit the feeders, Hutchinson says. He adds that heat lamps can also be placed about six inches from the feeder, and hummingbirds will even feed from these lamp-heated (and -lit) feeders at night. Some Seattle residents, he notes, have discovered that putting a drop or two of glycerin into the sugar water substantially reduces the temperature at which the liquid freezes; this can be used as an interim measure when a cold snap hits.

No matter which type of hummingbird feeder you have, how many of them you decide to use, and where you place them around your garden, these feeders are sure to bring you closer to the hummingbirds, and they to you.

Perhaps one day—like one hummingbird gardener I visited, whose hilltop terrace overlooking the sparkling Pacific Ocean in southern California featured three hummingbird feeders that were placed in a line and were hung about ten feet from each other—you will enjoy the pleasure of seeing not just one or two, but ten or twenty hummingbirds (of various species, if you live in the West) utilizing your feeders at the same time.

During my brief visit on this terrace in early February, I saw no less than ten or twelve hummingbirds continually swarming to the feeders, including mostly male and female Anna's Hummingbirds as well as a male Costa's Hummingbird and a male Allen's Hummingbird.

At one point, six Anna's Hummingbirds were visiting one of these eight-holed, flying-saucer-shaped feeders at the same time, some perching or hovering, with their bills buried deep in the holes, some approaching the feeder from the side, and others hovering just above the holes, ready to drop down for a drink.

At this point, caught up in the beauty of the moment, all I could think of were the words, "This is what having a hummingbird garden is all about!"

Indeed, as we'll see in the next chapter, there are many interesting events and activities, generated both by humans and by hummingbirds, that are likely to occur in hummingbird gardens across the country.

1. Chinese lantern
(Abutilon hybridum)
bushes.

2. Ruby-throated
Hummingbird
nest, in an
eastern red-
cedar *(Juniperus
virginiana)* tree.

3. Adult male
Anna's Humming-
bird, perched
on a pyracantha
branch.

4. Anna's Humming-
bird, nectaring
on pink powder
puff *(Calliandra
haematocephala)*.

5. Adult male
Costa's Humming-
bird, cleaning his
bill on a branch.

6. Adult male Costa's
Hummingbird.

7. Anna's Humming-
bird, nectaring on
tree aloe *(Aloe
arborescens)*.

8. Adult male Costa's
Hummingbird,
nectaring on
bladderpod
(Isomeris arborea),
but using his feet
for a momentary
perch.

9. Adult male Costa's
Hummingbird,
nectaring on
bladderpod
(Isomeris arborea).

10. Rufous or Allen's hummingbird (females and immatures of the
two are almost identical in the field), in a patch of scarlet
penstemon *(Penstemon labrosus).*

11. Woolly blue curls *(Trichostema lanatum),* a popular hummingbird
wildflower.

12. Rufous or Allen's hummingbird, nectaring on Cape honeysuckle *(Tecomaria capensis).*

13. Anna's Hummingbird, nectaring on Cape honeysuckle *(Tecomaria capensis).*

14. Anna's Hummingbird, nectaring on lantana *(Lantana camara).*

15. Garden scene:
Chinese lantern
(Abutilon hybridum
'Vesuvius Red').

16. Immature male
Anna's Humming-
bird, at feeder.

17. Immature male
Anna's Humming-
bird, at feeder.

18. Garden scene: common foxglove *(Digitalis purpurea)*.

19. Garden scene: Chinese lantern 'Vesuvius Red,' Chinese hibiscus, lemon tree, impatiens, all of which provide nectar to hummingbirds.

20. Garden scene: blood-red trumpet vine, Canterbury bell, nasturtium, snapdragon, azalea, petunia; coral tree in background.

7

Hummingbird
Garden
Activities

M y backyard, in the Brentwood section of Los Angeles, consists of a corner area bounded on two sides by a fifteen-
foot-tall Victorian box hedge intertwined with Cape honeysuckle, blood-red trumpet vine, and pink bougainvillea.
A tall red-ironbark eucalyptus stands out from the corner, towering over
a low row of 'Meyer' lemon and limequat shrubs. In the eastern corner of
the south hedge, the Victorian box has grown to a height of about thirty
feet, and it towers over everything else in the yard, except the eucalyptus
tree.

Looking south from my picture window, I can observe the varied
activities of at least five species of regular avian visitors to a rectangular
glass baking dish that sits atop a post three and a half feet tall in the
middle of the lawn and serves as a bird feeder. While such birds as the
scrub jay, house finch, mockingbird, mourning dove, and house sparrow
peck away at the birdseed that the owners of this property provide for
them, the familiar "whzz-whzz-whzz" and short chips of a male Anna's
Hummingbird can often be heard (along with the assorted calls of these
other birds) as it gleans nectar from the pink-flowering eucalyptus when
it's in bloom, and the Cape honeysuckle, which is always in bloom here.

Since I am not the owner of this property, I do not have a hummingbird garden per se, but I did discover that by hanging a hummingbird feeder about fifteen feet away from my window (and about six feet high on the eastern hedge of Victorian box), I was able to attract an immature male Anna's Hummingbird the very next day (see Photos 16 and 17). (In your garden, you could plant a row of foxglove, bee balm, or penstemon—or use all three of these hummingbird plants, as well as a hummingbird feeder—for the same effect.)

By providing a reliable source of nectar for this hummingbird, I have been able to observe the intricacies of its behavior, starting from the moment it chanced upon the feeder.

The most amazing thing about this process, to me, was just how quickly this hummingbird established this corner of the yard as his domain, not only with respect to other hummingbirds, but even in relation to the larger birds that also visit the yard (and, after all, were here first)—and even in relation to me.

For instance, the very afternoon that this hummingbird discovered the feeder (less than twenty-four hours after I had set it up), he seemed perfectly at home with it, as if he had used this type of feeder before, perhaps in some other yard.

I immediately went inside the guesthouse that I occupy here, grabbed my camera, and came back and positioned myself about seven feet from the feeder, in order to get a good close-up shot of the feeder and the bird. But this did not deter this feisty hummingbird from visiting the feeder. He just positioned himself on the far side of the feeder, and bobbed his head up from time to time, in order to keep an eye on what I was doing. Each time he bobbed up and down like this, he would chip a few times, as if to keep me at bay, and each time he returned to one of his various perches in the yard, he would "whzz-whzz-whzz" wildly (especially just before and just after visiting the feeder), as if to make it clear, in no uncertain terms, that this was his yard now, and this was his feeder—and let any intruder, large or small, beware.

But mere familiarity with his surroundings wasn't enough for this hummingbird. Once, on this first afternoon, I flushed the hummingbird away from the feeder by getting up too rapidly from a seated position nearby. He immediately retreated to a bare branch on the Victorian box just a few feet away, and started chip-chip-chipping ferociously at me, as if I had disturbed his dinner. An hour later, I was making a minor adjustment in the position of the feeder for my photographs, and the hummingbird flew directly to a wire just above the hedge (and directly over the feeder), and again started chipping wildly (angrily?) at me. When I retreated, he came down to the feeder and started to drink.

The next day, a similar sequence of events occurred, as the hummingbird became more and more used to using his feeder. Once a rival hummingbird tried to force him off of his perch on the nearby bare branch by swinging just overhead in a wide, low, U-shaped arc. But my hummingbird stood his ground, and the intruder was forced to establish a feeding territory of his own elsewhere. Later that day, he chased another interloper across the yard to the west, chipping wildly, and then retired about twenty feet high into the Victorian box to the south, and started to "whzz-whzz-whzz" from up there.

While he was perched up in the Victorian box, about thirty feet away from my porch, I got out my 8 × 30 Zeiss binoculars and began observing and taking copious notes regarding a peaceful perching interlude of twenty minutes in which he alternately scratched his beak and chin with each foot, preened his chest feathers and primaries with his beak, and stretched out his wings and tail feathers from time to time. After coming down to the feeder for a drink, he returned to this perching area and clung to a tiny, bare limb with his little feet; this time, he didn't scratch or preen himself for a good ten minutes or so, before chasing off a group of about ten bushtits that had suddenly infiltrated his perching area in the Victorian box (and indeed, the yard). After a quick time-out for a drink at the feeder and a brief foray to chase a few of the straggling bushtits out of the eucalyptus tree, he suddenly appeared hovering high above a scrub jay that was perched on the wire above the feeder. After dive-bombing past the jay a couple of times, forcing the jay to abandon its perch on the wire, he returned to one of his favorite perches high up in the eucalyptus tree. The yard was clear of other birds now, and he was chipping and "whzz-whzz-whzzing" away up there, as if in celebration of this fact (or perhaps out of exasperation).

But the following day, something *truly* extraordinary happened. I was fiddling with the position of the feeder on the Victorian box branch, which contains some leaves at the end of it that cast an assortment of ever-changing shadows on the feeder, depending on the position of the sun. This is very good for keeping the sugar water in the feeder out of full sunlight most of the time, and will prolong its useful life for the hummingbirds—but it wreaks havoc on trying to get a good photograph of a hummingbird and the feeder in direct sunlight. So I tied a piece of string to one of these leafy stems and pulled the stem back by winding the string around a stem on the inside part of the hedge. Just as I was doing this, with my arm held over the feeder as if I were a lamppost, in came my hummingbird, chipping away in some amount of distress at this new change in the landscape.

But did he retreat when he saw me? Not in the least. In fact, he flew over so that he was hovering right in front of me, changing his position ever so slightly, and chipping away at me, as if to say, "What or who are you, and what are you doing here?" I remained motionless, and the hummingbird flew then to the feeder, perched on it, and started drinking away as I held my arm over the whole affair and watched the hummingbird out of the corner of my eye. The amazing thing that struck me just then, as I watched him drinking just inches away from me, was just how small he was—about the size of my thumb—for all the intricacy of his behavior.

After he was finished with the feeder, the hummingbird flew high up to his favorite perching area in the Victorian box, and then he immediately started chipping away again, as usual. I went back to fiddling with the string, and ten minutes later, the hummingbird visited the feeder again, this time perching at the artificial flower head right in front of me so that his back was to me as he drank, no more than six inches away. Every few sips or so, he lifted his head and turned it so that his eye was facing mine for just a moment. Reassured that everything was in order, he then went back to his feeding. After he finished drinking this time and returned to his perch in the Victorian box, I could only stand there in wonder, marveling at the tiny creature's trust that I would do it no harm.

Whether or not he knows that I am the provider of his nectar is impossible to tell (I presume that he does), but it is abundantly clear that he shows no fear of me—just the normal wariness that any wild animal has in any of his surroundings if he wishes to survive for a long time. Meanwhile, I've already become accustomed to seeing this hummingbird in my yard, even after only a few days of having him here, and I couldn't in good conscience take down the feeder now, so I guess I'm stuck with my hummingbird pet, and he with me, unless he decides to leave the premises, which he seems highly unlikely to do.

In your own yard, you can enjoy many hours of making similar observations and having experiences like the ones I've just described, as long as the hummingbirds are close to you. In order to facilitate making close-up observations of these hummingbirds, you might want to try using a good pair of binoculars, such as the pair I mentioned earlier in this chapter. I have found these binoculars to be extremely effective at providing me with a strong magnification level as well as an adequate intake of light into the lenses. This latter feature is very important when I am observing the hummingbird in my yard when he's perched in an area of dense foliage, and it's also very helpful for observing this hummingbird during that hour or so just before it gets dark, after which time the hummingbird finally abandons the feeder for the day and retires to his roosting spot, which is probably somewhere in the yard.

Whether undertaken in your yard or in the field, the photography of hummingbirds (and indeed, of all nature) provides challenges and rewards of its own. Most of the close-up photographs of hummingbirds and flowers that you see in this book were taken from about seven feet away (and sometimes closer) with a Tamron 80–210mm zoom lens, mounted on a Honeywell Pentax camera. I used Ektachrome 100 HC film most of the time and set the zoom at 210 for the highest magnification possible with this lens. I usually set my aperture at f/3.8, creating a blurry background and thereby highlighting my subject as well as allowing me to shoot at 1/250 (or, preferably, 1/500) of a second whenever possible, in order to stop the motion of the bird's wings as much as I could in natural light.

All of these photographs, except for Photo 3, were taken with a hand-held camera. Photo 3 was taken with a Nikkor 300mm lens, along with an extension tube and a teleconverter, all of which I attached to a Nikon N2020 camera mounted on a tall tripod. With this setup, I was focusing on my subject from about ten feet away, but the increased magnification made the image of the bird about the same size that my usual method did, and I'm very pleased with the results of using both of these techniques.

The use of the right film is extremely important in the photography of hummingbirds, as it is with most subjects. I found the ISO 100 film gave me the level of detail (i.e., fine grain) that I wanted, while still being "fast" enough (i.e., allowing in enough light) to enable me to shoot at a high shutter speed as often as possible.

As far as technique is concerned, the key word, as it is with most photographic endeavors, is patience, patience, and even more patience. Sometimes, you may have to stand (or, preferably, sit) in the same spot for two or three hours (or even the better part of a day) in order to be in the right place at the right time and under the best lighting conditions. By remaining in the same spot for a long period of time, the hummingbirds you are trying to photograph will become accustomed to your presence in their field of vision, and they will become increasingly more prone to fly over close to you.

If you stake yourself out in front of a plant, or even a specific flower head, and remain as motionless as possible for as long as you possibly can, sooner or later, a hummingbird should fly into your field of view. One thing that definitely doesn't work is to move toward a hummingbird. Unless it is facing away from you or is totally preoccupied with feeding at that very moment, you are almost certainly sure to scare it away in a hurry. But if you give yourself enough time to get what you want, sooner or later, the right opportunities should present themselves. Then, you must be prepared to take advantage of these opportunities. Otherwise, all of that waiting will be for naught.

Despite the difficulties, the exhilaration I have felt when snapping the shutter and knowing that I've captured the image to the best of my ability is worth all of the waiting. I am also acutely aware by now, after taking many hundreds of photographs of hummingbirds and the flowers on which they feed, that if I am fortunate enough to come up with just one photograph, out of a roll of thirty-six, that I consider to be excellent, then I am a very lucky photographer indeed. So if you endeavor to photograph hummingbirds, you should be prepared to take a few more photographs of each subject than you might think necessary, in order to get the best results that you possibly can.

Whether you attempt to photograph the hummingbirds in your yard (or elsewhere, for that matter), or you simply enjoy watching them with the naked eye, you can be sure of one thing regarding these fascinating creatures: There will always be plenty of activity.

But perhaps the most amazing thing that I ever saw in a hummingbird garden involved very little activity at all. Late one afternoon, I went over to visit a hummingbird gardener here in Los Angeles, and lo and behold, in this person's backyard, amid the penstemons and a series of hummingbird feeders, an Anna's Hummingbird female had built a nest in a California white oak, in which to raise her young.

When I arrived, the female was momentarily away from the nest, and I had an opportunity to step up onto a nearby bench and look over the top of the nest, which was placed on a shaded branch about seven feet off the ground. Inside, all I could see were the yellowish orange, gaping beaks of the two nestlings, who were eagerly waiting to be fed by their mother.

My host and I went away from the nest for a while, and when I next returned to it, darkness had fallen, and the female had returned to the nest to brood her young. There she sat, peacefully, in the glistening reflection of the garden's floodlights, her tiny body entirely filling the nest, and her tail, beak, and wings partially protruding from the front, back, and sides of this downy, lichen-covered structure.

She just sat there, quietly, hardly moving, with such dignity, and such a sense of purpose, and she jostled herself slightly every now and then, in order to make herself more comfortable. It was remarkable to me to think that all of this drama that was presenting itself in front of me—the development of a family of living, breathing things—was taking place within an area the approximate diameter of a quarter.

But perhaps this is why most people react to hummingbirds in the way that they do—precisely because these animals are so very small, and yet so very complex. Maybe we sense in them a certain humility, and smallness, that we feel about ourselves in the wide scheme of nature, and so we can relate to these tiny birds, and can empathize with their fragility as they combat the elements of nature and sometimes are forced to cross great distances in order to survive.

Whatever the reason for this connection between people and hummingbirds, it is a profound one, and you will certainly experience it if you care to lure these birds into your garden. Perhaps by so doing you will develop a relationship with a single hummingbird, or a group of different individuals, even over a period of years.

Then you will be treated to a series of images as the hummingbirds bob from one flower to the next, pivoting in midair and streaking off across the yard to take a rest on their favorite perch.

What better reward is there for a hummingbird gardener than a spectacle such as this?

8

Conservation of Hummingbirds

As we discussed earlier in this book, many of the hummingbird species that we see in the United States also occur, especially in winter, in Mexico and Central America.

Indeed, the Ruby-throated Hummingbird can be seen during the winter not only in much of Mexico, but (going progressively south) in all of Belize, Guatemala, El Salvador, Honduras, Nicaragua, Costa Rica, and about half of Panama.

Thus, whatever happens to the habitats of the Rubythroat, as well as those of the other hummingbirds that spend the winter in Mexico and Central America, will have a profound effect on the hummingbirds that residents of the United States and Canada eventually see in the spring and summer, as well as on the endemic hummingbird species (and other wildlife) in the former areas.

According to hummingbird expert F. Gary Stiles, even an ecologically aware Central American nation such as Costa Rica "has lost over half of its forests since 1940, and the remaining unprotected forest areas are suffering rapid attrition."

Ironically, Dr. Stiles tells me, "the clearing of forest may even have favored Rubythroats over many native species.

"Ruby-throated Hummingbirds do just fine in second-growth

scrub and coffee plantations with shade trees, such as *Inga* and *Erythrina,* in winter," he states, "though they can't make it in cotton fields or pastures.

"Hence," he goes on, "Rubythroats are not hurting for winter habitat, except in such areas as lowland El Salvador, where cotton monocultures have become widespread."

Nevertheless, Stiles reports that in Costa Rica, "only the national parks and wildlife refuges as well as certain private reserves are receiving anything like adequate protection. Within a very few years," he adds, "virtually all of Costa Rica's remaining forests may be in such areas."

It seems clear, as we move into the 1990s, that the natural habitats for hummingbirds (and indeed, for all forms of wildlife) from Mexico to Panama (and indeed, throughout North America) will have to be watched diligently and protected from the ravages of lumbering, land development, and agricultural clearing, while at the same time, the preservation of these natural areas as magnets for tourism, as internationally recognized and supported scientific "laboratories," and as areas with intrinsic value in perpetuating the diversity of life forms on earth should be a top priority in all countries.

Indeed, while the tropical rain forests and other habitats for overwintering North American hummingbirds are under an increasing threat of destruction today, the spread of urban development in the United States, while not threatening the survival of any one hummingbird species, continues to have an effect on local populations of hummingbirds.

As stated earlier, the Anna's Hummingbird (as well as the Rufoustailed Hummingbird *[Amazilia tzacatl]* in Central America) has been expanding its range due to its easy adaptation to a growing supply of suburban garden environments.

Hummingbird gardeners in urban, suburban, and rural areas across the United States can help to support local populations of all hummingbirds that are affected by changes in their natural environment.

In addition to planting your garden in order to support the hummingbirds in your area, you might want to become involved with some of the conservation organizations that are listed at the end of this book.

Indeed, whether you are working to protect a pocket of rain forest in Central America, a pristine canyon within a few miles of your suburban home, or even a well-planted park in the middle of a great city, you can help to preserve valuable habitats that will be utilized not only by hummingbirds but by a host of other animals as well.

In spite of conservation efforts, the International Council for Bird Preservation included 29 hummingbirds in its 1988 *World Checklist of Threatened Birds,* including Costa Rica's Mangrove Hummingbird *(Amazilia boucardi),* which is protected in the mangroves of the Corcovado National Park, located on the Pacific coast of that country.

Two other hummingbirds with the dubious distinction of being included on this list are the Bee Hummingbird of Cuba, which at two and one-quarter inches in length and less than two grams in weight is the smallest bird in the world; and the Marvelous Spatuletail of Peru, that wonderfully unique creature photographed for the first time in color by Crawford Greenewalt, and referred to in Chapter 1 of this text.

It would be a shame if creatures of this order of uniqueness (or any species of plant or animal), were wiped off the face of the earth forever, before or after we have had a chance to study them thoroughly.

It has been said many times in recent years that the threatened and endangered plants and animals of the world are a barometer of man's own ability to keep himself alive in the long run.

This is certainly as true with hummingbirds as it is with any other type of creature, for if we can allow a species such as the Bee Hummingbird or the Marvelous Spatuletail to fall by the wayside of evolution on earth, what does that really say about our ability to take care of anything in this world that has both beauty and grace?

It is to be hoped that hummingbird gardeners will play a role in preserving the populations of hummingbirds throughout the New World. Along the way, they're sure to be rewarded with plenty of hours of entertaining events in their yards to observe and lots of magical moments to remember.

So why not get out your trowel and plant a pineapple sage or two? The hummingbirds are waiting!

Fifteen Garden
Hummingbirds

The following list contains information about the fifteen species of hummingbirds that breed regularly in the United States and Canada. Depending on the region in which you live, you may have a good chance of attracting any of these hummingbirds to your garden.

Allen's Hummingbird *(Selasphorus sasin)*

Description: Males have a green back and crown, with a red throat, white breast, and rufous sides, rump, and tail. Females are green above, with red flecks on the throat, a white breast, and rufous sides. Size: 3″–3¾″.

Range: Along the West Coast, from southern Oregon to southern California.

Favorite Flowers: Columbine, hedge nettle, ceanothus, monkeyflower, tree tobacco, California fuchsia, penstemon, paintbrush, morning glory, madrone, lupine, agave, eucalyptus, honeysuckle, sage, Cape honeysuckle.

Season: January–September; resident subspecies *(S. s. sedentarius)* year-round in southern California.

Nesting: February–June.

Winters: Northwestern Mexico.

Migration Route: Southern California and Arizona; more coastal in spring, mainly through mountains in fall.

Habitats: Brushlands (especially coastal sage scrub), woodlands, canyons, gardens, parks, mountain meadows (later in season).

Special Features: Adult male looks similar to the Rufous Hummingbird, but the Rufous has a rufous back; females of the two species look almost identical. Wings of males trill in flight, as do those of Rufous males. Outermost tail feathers of males vibrate in display. Calls: a buzzy "zeee" and a quick "chuppity-chup."

Anna's Hummingbird *(Calypte anna)*

Description: Males have a green back, with a red throat and crown. Females are green above, often with a small patch of red on the throat. Both sexes have lightish gray and green undersides. Size: 3½"–4¼".

Range: California, Arizona, expanding into Pacific Northwest; accidental in some other western states.

Favorite Flowers: Chinese lantern, fuchsia, Cape honeysuckle, lantana, eucalyptus, bottlebrush, fuchsia-flowering gooseberry, tree tobacco, red-hot poker, citrus, monkeyflower, acacia, foxglove, geranium, red cestrum, pink powder puff, agave, columbine, blood-red trumpet vine, paintbrush, bird of paradise, California fuchsia, manzanita, lupine, Indian pink, sky-rocket, ceanothus, coral tree, chuparosa, scarlet delphinium, lily-of-the-Nile, chasmanthe, aloe.

Season: Year-round in most areas.

Nesting: November–August.

Winters: Resident throughout most of range. Some wintering populations occur in southern Arizona, Sonora and Baja California in Mexico, and the Pacific Northwest.

Migration Route: No regular migrations, but will move higher into mountains in summer and fall.

Habitats: Chaparral, canyons, woodlands, gardens, mountains.

Special Features: This hummingbird is extending its year-round range northward and eastward, primarily because of suburban plantings and hummingbird feeders in these areas. Males are pugnacious and have the closest thing to a hummingbird song. In addition to this scratchy "song," males have a spectacular, steep diving display, used mainly as an aggressive display, but also as a courtship display.

Black-chinned Hummingbird *(Archilochus alexandri)*

Description: Males have a dark-green back and crown, with a purple band at the base of the black throat, a white breast, and green sides. Females have a green back and crown, may have small dark spots on the whitish throat, and have a white underside and a hint of buff on the flanks. Size: 3¼″−3¾″.

Range: Throughout most of western U.S., from western Texas to British Columbia. Not present on Pacific Northwest coast.

Favorite Flowers: Honeysuckle, sage, ocotillo, tree tobacco, nasturtium, chuparosa, shrimp plant, lantana, petunia, palo verde, butterfly bush, bird of paradise, scarlet delphinium, citrus, jasmine, paintbrush, hollyhock, columbine, agave, gilia, gladiolus, penstemon, yucca, canna, fuchsia-flowering gooseberry, red-flowering currant, aloe.

Season: March−October.

Nesting: April−July.

Winters: Mostly in Mexico, but some individuals spend the winter in southern Texas and along the Gulf Coast. Very rare in southern California in winter.

Migration Route: From wintering grounds in Mexico to U.S. range.

Habitats: Streamside and oak woodlands, canyons, mountainsides, chaparral, parks, gardens, deserts (during migration).

Special Features: Closely related and similar in appearance to the Ruby-throated Hummingbird (females are almost identical). Males give a dry buzz in flight. Their display is a rapid, pendulumlike arc.

Blue-throated Hummingbird *(Lampornis clemenciae)*

Description: Males have a green back and crown, with a blue throat and gray underside. Females have a green back and crown, with a gray throat and gray underside. Both sexes have long, broad, black tails with much white in corners. Size: 4½″−5½″.

Range: Southeastern Arizona, southern New Mexico, and western Texas (especially the Chisos Mountains).

Favorite Flowers: Gilia, sage, penstemon, agave, columbine, lobelia, honeysuckle, California fuchsia.

Season: March—October.

Nesting: April—July.

Winters: Mostly in Mexico, although some individuals spend the winter north of the Mexican border.

Migration Route: From wintering grounds in Mexico to U.S. range.

Habitats: Streamsides of mountain canyons and valleys, gardens.

Special Features: Females return to the same nesting sites from year to year and often build new nests on top of the old ones. The Blue-throated and Magnificent hummingbirds are the largest hummingbirds that breed north of Mexico. Call is a sharp "seeep!" frequently repeated.

Broad-billed Hummingbird *(Cynanthus latirostris)*

Description: Males have a green back and crown, with a blue throat and green underside. Females have a green back and crown and have a gray throat and underside. Both sexes have a red bill with a black tip and a broad, blue-black tail. Size: 3¼"–4".

Range: Southern Arizona, southwestern New Mexico, and western Texas.

Favorite Flowers: Ocotillo, honeysuckle, cactus, agave, scarlet bouvardia, paintbrush, butterfly weed, penstemon.

Season: March—October.

Nesting: April—August.

Winters: Mexico; uncommonly in southern Arizona, casually in California.

Migration Route: From wintering grounds in Mexico to U.S. range; straggler to California, mainly from September—April.

Habitats: Desert canyons, streamsides, mountainsides, woodlands, scrublands, gardens. Likes mesquite-sycamore vegetation.

Special Features: Red bill is readily observable, even from a distance. Call is a rapid, chattering "chi-dit" or "ji-dit."

Broad-tailed Hummingbird *(Selasphorus platycercus)*

Description: Males have a green back and crown, with a rose-red throat, a white underside, and green sides. Females have a green back and crown, dark spots on the throat, a white underside, and light-rufous sides. Size: 3¾"–4½".

Range: Most of western U.S. (except West Coast), including Rocky Mountains, Great Basin, Arizona, New Mexico, western Texas, and eastern California.

Favorite Flowers: Penstemon, ocotillo, delphinium, cactus, nasturtium, skyrocket, agave, paintbrush, iris, lupine, New Mexico locust, sage, yucca, gilia, bee balm, fuchsia-flowering gooseberry.

Season: February–October.

Nesting: March–July.

Winters: Mexico.

Migration Route: From wintering grounds in Mexico, northward through western Texas and eastern New Mexico, to Rocky Mountains and adjoining areas.

Habitats: Mountain slopes, meadows, woodlands, streamsides, canyons, valleys, foothills, gardens.

Special Features: Adult males in flight produce a loud, cricketlike trilling sound with their feathers.

Buff-bellied Hummingbird *(Amazilia yucatanensis)*

Description: Males and females have green backs and crowns, with green throats and breasts, buff-brown undersides, and red, black-tipped bills. Size: 4"–4½".

Range: Gulf Coast from Louisiana to the southern tip of Texas (mostly from the central Texas coast south).

Favorite Flowers: Various trees and shrubs in the legume family, including honey mesquite, western coral bean, and Texas ebony; Texas mallow, anaqua.

Season: April–October, but many individuals spend the winter within the U.S. range.

Nesting: March–July.

Winters: Eastern Mexico, along the Gulf Coast.

Migration Route: From Mexican wintering grounds to U.S. range.

Habitats: Woodlands, scrublands, streamsides, pastures, gardens, citrus orchards, palm groves, wet thickets.

Special Features: Has a high, squeaky, metallic voice.

Calliope Hummingbird *(Stellula calliope)*

Description: Males have a green back and crown, with streaks of purplish red on the throat, a white breast, and greenish sides. Females are green above, with dark specks on the throat, a white breast, and light-rufous sides. Size: 2¾″–4″.

Range: Most of western U.S., from Rocky Mountains to Pacific Coast. Also occurs in British Columbia and Alberta.

Favorite Flowers: Paintbrush, manzanita, penstemon, columbine, citrus, sky-rocket, fuchsia-flowering gooseberry, monkeyflower, hawthorn, agave, dwarf lousewort, sage, snow plant, ceanothus, lupine.

Season: March–September.

Nesting: May–July.

Winters: Mexico.

Migration Route: Through Arizona and New Mexico to breeding grounds primarily in mountains of the West.

Habitats: Mountain forest edges, meadows, canyons, valleys, streamsides; lowlands and gardens during migration.

Special Features: Smallest hummingbird that breeds north of Mexico. Uniqueness of tiny size and streaked gorget make the Calliope a special hummingbird. Calls are very high-pitched. Female looks like a small Broad-tailed Hummingbird, with a relatively short bill and tail.

Costa's Hummingbird *(Calypte costae)*

Description: Males have a green back, purple crown and throat, are whitish below, and have green sides. The male's purple throat feathers extend greatly to the sides. Females have a green back and crown, and have a whitish throat and underside. Size: 3″–3½″.

Range: Southwestern U.S.

Favorite Flowers: Chuparosa, ocotillo, bladderpod, woolly blue curls, western redbud, desert willow, fuchsia-flowering gooseberry, sage, agave, penstemon, scarlet delphinium, butterfly weed, apricot, cherry, plum.

Season: Resident throughout most of its range; early spring migrants arrive by late January, return to wintering grounds by October.

Nesting: January–June.

Winters: Many individuals spend the winter in northwest Mexico.

Migration Route: From wintering grounds in Mexico to U.S. range (limited migratory movements).

Habitats: Deserts, chaparral, scrublands, canyons, parks, gardens.

Special Features: Resident populations have increased in recent years, as the Costa's has taken advantage of cultivated plantings in urbanized areas. Desert populations nest earlier than coastal ones. The male's display call is a very high-pitched whine.

Lucifer Hummingbird *(Calothorax lucifer)*

Description: Males have a green back and crown, with a purple throat, a whitish underside, and green and rusty sides. Females have a green back and crown, with a light-brown throat and underside. Both sexes have a decurved bill. Size: 3¼″–3¾″.

Range: Chisos Mountains of western Texas; uncommonly in southeastern Arizona.

Favorite Flowers: Agave, coral tree, lupine, sage, ocotillo, tree tobacco.

Season: March–November.

Nesting: May–August.

Winters: Mexico.

Migration Route: From wintering grounds in Mexico to U.S. range.

Habitats: Deserts, canyons, scrublands, gardens.

Special Features: This spectacular-looking hummingbird is especially fond of environments that feature agave flowers. It's most easily seen in Big Bend National Park, but is also a regular visitor to gardens in Portal, Arizona, and adjoining areas. Its distinctly curved bill is unique among U.S. hummingbirds.

Magnificent Hummingbird *(Eugenes fulgens)*

Description: Males have a dark-green back and a purple crown, with a brilliant green throat and a blackish underside. Females have a green back and crown, spots on the throat, and a grayish underside. Both sexes have a white spot behind the eye. Size: 4½"–5½".

Range: Southeastern Arizona, southwestern New Mexico, Chisos Mountains of western Texas.

Favorite Flowers: Agave, monkeyflower, honeysuckle, penstemon, sage, coral tree, lobelia, iris, columbine, fuchsia, geranium.

Season: April–November.

Nesting: May–July.

Winters: Mexico.

Migration Route: From Mexican wintering grounds to U.S. range.

Habitats: Mountains, canyons, woodlands, meadows, streamsides, parks, gardens; lowlands, rarely during migration.

Special Features: A strikingly large and brilliant hummingbird, this species wanders northward to Colorado in summer after breeding. Formerly called Rivoli's Hummingbird.

Ruby-throated Hummingbird *(Archilochus colubris)*

Description: Males have a green back and crown, with a red throat, a whitish underside, and some green on sides. Females are green above, may have small dark spots on the whitish throat, and have a whitish underside, and a touch of cinnamon on the flanks. Size: 3"–3¾".

Range: From eastern U.S. and Canada, westward to Alberta in north, south across Great Plains to eastern Texas.

Favorite Flowers: Jewelweed, bee balm, trumpet creeper, coral bells, columbine, morning glory, honeysuckle, fire pink, nasturtium, cardinal flower, sage, gladiolus, dahlia, butterfly bush, lantana, four o'clock, delphinium, petunia, red buckeye, weigela, hibiscus, phlox, red-hot poker, lily, snapdragon, foxglove, citrus, silktree, paintbrush, scarlet gilia, fuchsia, nicotiana, beauty bush, coral bean, Indian pink, Siberian peashrub, golden currant, thistle, black locust.

Season: March–October, year-round in some parts of the extreme South.

Nesting: March–July.

Winters: Mexico south to Panama; some individuals spend the winter in southern Florida and Gulf Coast.

Migration Route: Some individuals take the overland route from Mexico through Texas; many cross the Gulf of Mexico in a remarkable nonstop flight.

Habitats: Woodlands, meadows, streamsides, parks, gardens.

Special Features: Probably the best-known and longest-studied North American hummingbird, no doubt because of its historic association with European settlers, up to the present time. The only hummingbird through most of eastern U.S. and Canada.

Rufous Hummingbird *(Selasphorus rufus)*

Description: Males have a rufous back, rump, and tail, a green crown, a red throat, white breast, and rufous sides. Females are green above, with specks of red on the throat, a white breast, and rufous sides. Size: 3"–4".

Range: Most of western U.S., northward through British Columbia to southeastern Alaska; occasionally along Gulf Coast from Texas to Florida, later in year. Breeds from Oregon and Idaho north.

Favorite Flowers: Fuchsia-flowering gooseberry, red-flowering currant, madrone, manzanita, lungwort, honeysuckle, columbine, Rocky Mountain bee plant, ocotillo, agave, penstemon, paintbrush, fuchsia, eucalyptus, citrus, lily, geranium, ceanothus, tree tobacco, lantana, delphinium, hibiscus, lupine, red-hot poker, silktree, gilia, skyrocket, nasturtium, bee balm, fireweed, petunia, hollyhock, yucca, nicotiana, sage, peach, Cape honeysuckle, thimbleberry, salmonberry.

Season: February–October.

Nesting: April–July.

Winters: Mexico, although some individuals spend the winter in southern California and along the Gulf Coast.

Migration Route: In spring, from Mexican wintering grounds northward primarily along the lowlands of the West Coast to breeding grounds in the Pacific Northwest; in fall, southward through inland mountain ranges, especially the Rocky Mountains.

Habitats: Woodlands, meadows, mountains, lowlands, chaparral, stream-sides, parks, gardens.

Special Features: Well-known for its aggressively territorial behavior toward other hummingbirds, and even birds much larger than itself, while defending its nesting and foraging areas. Males give a trilling sound in flight. Females and young males are generally indistinguishable from Allen's Hummingbirds.

Violet-crowned Hummingbird *(Amazilia violiceps)*

Description: Males have a bronze-green back and purple crown, with a white throat and underside. Females look similar to males, but have duller crowns. Both sexes have a red bill with a black tip. Size: 3¾"–4½".

Range: Southeastern Arizona, southwestern New Mexico.

Favorite Flowers: Agave, honey mesquite, paintbrush, sage, penstemon, columbine, Texas betony.

Season: May–September.

Nesting: June–July.

Winters: Mexico.

Migration Route: From wintering grounds in Mexico to U.S. range.

Habitats: Canyons, streamsides, sycamore groves, woodlands, parks, gardens.

Special Features: Only U.S. hummingbird with completely white underside. Call is a quick, chattering note. Has straggled west to California.

White-eared Hummingbird *(Hylocharis leucotis)*

Description: Males have a green back and a purple crown, with a blue-green throat and a green underside. Females have a green back and crown, with green spots on the throat, a white underside, and green-spotted sides. Both sexes have a thin, white band that proceeds back from just above the eyes, and both sexes also have a red bill with a black tip. Size: 3½"–3¾".

Range: Southeastern Arizona, southwestern New Mexico, and the Chisos Mountains of western Texas, mainly as a nonbreeding visitor.

Favorite Flowers: Honeysuckle, scarlet bouvardia, agave, penstemon, sage, lobelia.

Season: April–October.

Nesting: Does not normally breed in the U.S. part of its range.

Winters: Mexico.

Migration Route: From wintering grounds in Mexico to U.S. range.

Habitats: Mountain woodlands, canyons, meadows, streamsides, parks, gardens.

Special Features: Recent records indicate that this species is starting to breed within parts of its U.S. range. Call is a continuous ticking sound.

Cultivated Flowers

Abelia, glossy *(Abelia grandiflora)* shrub; white, pink; June–October.

Acacia *(Acacia)* shrub, tree; yellow; mostly in spring.

Aechmea *(Aechmea)* bromeliad; red, blue, yellow; various times throughout year.

Agave *(Agave)* succulent; yellowish green; various times throughout year.

Aloe *(Aloe)* succulent; red, orange, yellow, white; various times throughout year.

Aloe, tree *(Aloe arborescens)* succulent; red; December–February.

Amethyst flower *(Browallia)* annual, sometimes perennial; blue, purple, white; summer, sometimes longer.

Anaqua *(Ehretia anacua)* shrub, tree; white; late winter–spring, sometimes in fall.

Aphelandra *(Aphelandra)* houseplant, occasionally grown outdoors in warmer areas; red, yellow, orange, white; various times throughout year.

Apple; crabapple *(Malus)* tree; pink, red, white; spring.

Apricot *(Prunus armeniaca)* tree; pink, white; spring.

Australian fuchsia *(Correa)* shrub; pink, red, greenish yellow, white; fall–spring, sometimes longer.

Azalea *(Rhododendron)* shrub; various colors; early spring–summer.

Balloon flower *(Platycodon grandiflorus)* perennial; blue, June–August.

Balsam *(Impatiens balsamina)* annual; red, white, pink, purple; summer.

Banana *(Musa)* clump-forming perennial; yellow, orange; various times throughout year.

Beauty bush *(Kolkwitzia amabilis)* shrub; pink; May–June.

Begonia *(Begonia)* perennial; various colors; most of year.

Bellflower *(Campanula)* perennial, biennial, annual; blue, purple, white, pink; spring–fall.

Bird of paradise *(Strelitzia reginae)* perennial; orange, blue, and white; various times throughout year.

Bird of paradise bush *(Caesalpinia gilliessi)* shrub or small tree; yellow; summer.

Bleeding heart, common *(Dicentra spectabilis)* perennial; pink; late spring.

Blood-red trumpet vine *(Distictis buccinatoria)* vine; orange-red; various times throughout year.

Bottlebrush *(Callistemon)* shrub, tree; red; most of year.

Bougainvillea *(Bougainvillea)* vine; various colors; most of year.

Butterfly bush *(Buddleia davidii)* shrub; purple; summer.

Cactus *(Opuntia)* succulent; yellow, white, pale green; spring–early summer.

Cactus, Christmas *(Schlumbergera bridgesii)* succulent; red; winter.

Camellia *(Camellia)* shrub, small tree; various colors; fall–spring.

Canna *(Canna)* tuberous rootstock; various colors; summer–fall.

Canterbury bell *(Campanula medium)* biennial; purple, blue, pink, white, lavender; early summer.

Cape honeysuckle *(Tecomaria capensis)* vine, shrub; orange-red; fall–spring, sometimes longer.

Carpet bugle *(Ajuga reptans)* perennial; blue; spring–early summer.

Catmint *(Nepeta faassenii)* perennial; blue; early summer.

Catnip *(Nepeta cataria)* perennial; white, lavender; June.

Ceanothus *(Ceanothus)* shrub, small tree, ground cover; blue, white, purple; spring.

Century plant *(Agave americana)* succulent; yellowish green; various times throughout year.

Cestrum, red *(Cestrum elegans)* shrub; red; spring–summer.

Chasmanthe *(Chasmanthe aethiopica)* corm; orange-red; spring–summer.

Chaste tree *(Vitex agnus-castus)* shrub or small tree; blue, white, pink; summer–fall.

Cherry *(Prunus)* tree; white, pink; spring.

Chinaberry *(Melia azedarach)* tree; lilac; spring–early summer.

Chinese lantern *(Abutilon hybridum)* shrub; pink, yellow, white, red; most of year (see Photo 15).

Cigar plant *(Cuphea ignea)* perennial; red; summer–fall.

Citrus *(Citrus)* tree, shrub; white; spring, sometimes longer.

Clematis *(Clematis)* vine; various colors; most of year.

Clematis, sweet autumn *(Clematis dioscoreifolia)* vine; white; late summer–fall.

Columbine *(Aquilegia)* perennial; various colors; spring–early summer.

Columnea *(Columnea)* houseplant, occasionally grown outdoors in warmer areas; red, orange, yellow; various times throughout year.

Coral fountain *(Russelia equisetiformis)* perennial; red; spring–summer, sometimes longer.

Coral tree *(Erythrina)* tree, shrub; red; most of year.

Crape myrtle *(Lagerstroemia indica)* shrub, tree; pink, red, purple, white; July–September.

Cup-of-gold vine *(Solandra maxima)* vine; yellow; various times throughout year.

Cypress vine *(Ipomoea quamoclit)* annual vine; red; summer.

Dahlia *(Dahlia)* perennial; various colors; summer–frost.

Daylily *(Hemerocallis fulva)* perennial; orange; summer.

Delphinium; larkspur *(Delphinium)* perennial, annual; various colors; spring–fall.

Dudleya *(Dudleya)* succulent; red, yellow; most of year.

Dwarf poinciana *(Caesalpina pulcherrima)* shrub; orange, red, yellow; year-round.

Eucalyptus *(Eucalyptus)* tree, shrub; white, red, yellow, pink, orange; various times throughout year.

Eucalyptus, bluegum *(Eucalyptus globulus)* tree; white; winter–spring.

Eucalyptus, red-ironbark *(Eucalyptus sideroxylon)* tree; pink; fall–summer.

Evening primrose *(Oenothera)* biennial, perennial; pink, yellow; various times throughout year.

False dragonhead *(Physostegia virginiana)* perennial; white, pink, purple; summer.

Flame vine *(Pyrostegia venusta)* vine; orange; fall–early winter.

Floss silk tree *(Chorisia speciosa)* tree; pink; fall.

Four o'clock *(Mirabilis jalapa)* perennial, sometimes treated as annual; red, pink, yellow, white; summer–fall.

Foxglove *(Digitalis)* biennial, perennial; various colors; summer.

Foxglove, common *(Digitalis purpurea)* biennial, perennial; purple, white, pink, red, yellow; summer (see Photo 18).

Fuchsia *(Fuchsia)* shrub; pink, purple, red, sometimes with white; early summer–frost, sometimes longer.

Geranium *(Pelargonium)* perennial; red, white, pink, purple, orange; spring–fall.

Gilia *(Gilia)* annual; blue, purple; summer.

Gladiolus *(Gladiolus)* corm; various colors; spring–fall.

Globe thistle *(Echinops exaltatus)* perennial; blue; midsummer–late fall.

Glorybower, bleeding heart *(Clerodendrum thomsoniae)* vine; red and white; August–October.

Grevillea *(Grevillea)* shrub, tree; red, yellow, white, pink, orange; various times throughout year.

Ground ivy, or gill-over-the-ground *(Glechoma hederacea)* perennial; blue, purple; spring–summer.

Guzmania *(Guzmania)* bromeliad; yellow, white; various times throughout year.

Hawthorn *(Crataegus)* tree; white; spring–early summer.

Heliconia *(Heliconia)* clump-forming perennial; red, yellow, white, orange, green; various times throughout year.

Hibiscus, Chinese *(Hibiscus rosa-sinensis)* shrub; red, white, pink, yellow, orange; summer.

Hollyhock *(Alcea rosea)* biennial, sometimes treated as short-lived perennial; red, white, pink, purple, yellow; summer.

Honeysuckle *(Lonicera)* shrub, vine; white, red, yellow, purple, pink; spring–frost.

Honeysuckle, Japanese *(Lonicera japonica)* vine; white, then yellow; spring–summer, sometimes longer.

Horsechestnut, common *(Aesculus hippocastanum)* tree; white; spring.

Horsechestnut, red *(Aesculus carnea)* tree; red, pink; spring.

Hosta *(Hosta)* perennial; lavender, white, blue, purple; summer.

Hummingbird bush *(Grevillea thelemannia)* shrub; red; various times throughout year.

Impatiens *(Impatiens)* annual, perennial; red, white, pink, purple, orange; summer.

Iochroma *(Iochroma cyaneum)* shrub; blue, purple; summer.

Iris *(Iris)* bulb, rhizome; various colors; usually spring–summer, sometimes longer.

Island bush-snapdragon *(Galvezia speciosa)* shrub; red; various times throughout year.

Japanese aralia *(Fatsia japonica)* shrub; white; fall–winter.

Jasmine *(Jasminum)* shrub, vine; yellow, white, pink; spring–fall, sometimes longer.

Jerusalem thorn *(Parkinsonia aculeata)* tree; yellow; various times throughout year.

Kumquat *(Fortunella)* shrub, small tree; white; spring, sometimes longer.

Lantana *(Lantana)* shrub; red, yellow, pink, purple, orange; year-round in warmer areas.

Lavender, English *(Lavandula angustifolia)* shrub; lavender; summer.

Lemon *(Citrus limon)* tree, shrub; white; spring, sometimes longer.

Lilac *(Syringa)* shrub; various colors; spring–early summer.

Lily *(Lilium)* bulb; various colors; spring–fall.

Lily, tiger *(Lilium lancifolium)* bulb; orange; summer.

Lily-of-the-Nile *(Agapanthus)* perennial; blue, white; summer–early fall.

Limequat *(Citrofortunella)* shrub, small tree; white; spring, sometimes longer.

Lion's tail *(Leonotis leonurus)* perennial; orange; summer–fall.

Lobelia *(Lobelia)* perennial, annual; red, blue, purple, pink, white; early summer–frost.

Loquat *(Eriobotrya japonica)* tree; white; fall.

Lungwort *(Pulmonaria)* perennial; blue, purple, pink, white; spring.

Lupine *(Lupinus)* annual, perennial, shrub; various colors; spring–fall.

Madrone *(Arbutus menziesii)* tree, large shrub; white, pink; spring.

Maltese cross *(Lychnis chalcedonia)* perennial; red; summer.

Manzanita *(Arctostaphylos)* shrub, small tree; white, pink; December–April.

Melaleuca *(Melaleuca)* tree, shrub; white, pink, purple, red; most of year.

Mesquite, honey *(Prosopis glandulosa)* tree, large shrub; yellow; spring–summer.

Mint *(Mentha)* perennial; purple; summer.

Monkeyflower *(Mimulus)* perennial, sometimes treated as an annual; orange, yellow, pink, red; late spring–fall, often longer.

Montbretia *(Crocosmia crocosmiiflora)* corm; orange-red; summer–fall.

Morning glory *(Ipomoea)* vine; various colors; summer–frost.

Mullein pink, or rose campion *(Lychnis coronaria)* perennial; purplish red; spring–summer.

Nasturtium *(Tropaeolum majus)* annual, treated as perennial in warmer areas; orange, yellow, red, white; most of year (see Photo 20).

Nicotiana, or flowering tobacco *(Nicotiana)* perennial, treated as annual; white, red, pink, purple; summer.

Orange *(Citrus)* tree, shrub; white; spring, sometimes longer.

Palo verde *(Cercidium)* tree; yellow; spring, sometimes longer.

Peach; nectarine *(Prunus persica)* tree; pink, white; spring.

Penstemon, or beardtongue *(Penstemon)* perennial, shrub; various colors; spring–summer, sometimes longer.

Periwinkle *(Vinca major)* perennial; purplish blue; spring–summer, often longer.

Peruvian lily *(Alstroemeria psittacina)* perennial; red; May–midsummer.

Petunia *(Petunia)* perennial, treated as annual; various colors; spring–summer.

Phlox *(Phlox)* annual, perennial; various colors; spring–frost.

Pincushion flower *(Scabiosa)* annual, perennial; various colors; summer–frost, sometimes longer.

Pink *(Dianthus)* perennial, biennial, annual; various colors; spring–fall, sometimes longer.

Plum *(Prunus)* tree; white, pink; spring.

Powder puff, pink *(Calliandra haematocephala)* shrub; pink; fall–spring.

Primrose *(Primula)* perennial, sometimes treated as annual; various colors; various times throughout year.

Quince, flowering *(Chaenomeles)* shrub; white, pink, orange, red; late winter–early spring.

Red-hot poker *(Kniphofia uvaria)* perennial; orange-red; spring–frost, sometimes longer.

Rhododendron *(Rhododendron)* shrub; various colors; spring–summer.

Rosa de Montana *(Antigonon leptopus)* vine; pink; midsummer–fall.

Rose mallow *(Hibiscus moscheutos)* perennial; red, pink, white; early summer–frost.

Rose of Sharon *(Hibiscus syriacus)* shrub; purplish blue, white, red; summer.

Royal poinciana *(Delonix regia)* tree; red, orange, yellow and red; summer.

Sage *(Salvia)* annual, biennial, perennial, shrub; various colors; spring–frost.

Sage, garden *(Salvia officinalis)* perennial; purplish blue; early summer.

Sage, mealy-cup *(Salvia farinacea)* perennial, often treated as annual; purplish blue, blue, white; summer–fall.

Sage, Mexican bush *(Salvia leucantha)* shrub; purple; summer–fall.

Sage, pineapple *(Salvia elegans)* perennial; red; fall.

Sage, scarlet *(Salvia splendens)* annual; red, white, lavender; early summer–frost.

Salmonberry *(Rubus spectabilis)* shrub; purplish red; March–June.

Scarlet runner bean *(Phaseolus coccineus)* perennial vine, often grown as annual; red; midsummer–late summer.

Shrimp plant *(Justicia brandegeana)* shrub; white; spring–fall, sometimes longer.

Siberian peashrub *(Caragana arborescens)* shrub or small tree; yellow; spring.

Silktree, or mimosa *(Albizia julibrissin)* tree; pink; summer.

Snapdragon *(Antirrhinum)* perennial, usually treated as annual; various colors; most of year.

Sourwood *(Oxydendrum arboreum)* tree; white; midsummer–late summer.

Spider flower *(Cleome)* annual; pink, white, purple; midsummer–frost.

Spirea, or spiraea *(Spiraea bumalda)* shrub; red, pink, white; summer–fall.

Star clusters *(Pentas lanceolata)* perennial, usually treated as annual; white, red, purple, pink; various times throughout year.

Sweet William *(Dianthus barbatus)* biennial, often treated as annual; white, pink, purple, red, bicolored; summer.

Texas ebony *(Pithecellobium flexicaule)* tree, shrub; yellow; spring–summer.

Thimbleberry *(Rubus parviflorus)* shrub; white; March–August.

Tillandsia *(Tillandsia)* bromeliad; various colors; various times throughout year.

Toadflax *(Linaria marocanna)* annual; various colors; spring–frost, sometimes longer.

Trailing abutilon *(Abutilon megapotamicum)* shrub; red and yellow; May–October.

Tree tobacco *(Nicotiana glauca)* shrub or small tree; yellow; April–November.

Tree mallow *(Lavatera assurgentiflora)* shrub; reddish purple; spring–fall, sometimes longer.

Tritonia *(Tritonia)* corm; orange-red; late spring–summer

Tuberose *(Polianthes tuberosa)* tuber; white; summer–fall.

Tulip tree *(Liriodendron tulipifera)* tree; greenish yellow; spring.

Verbena *(Verbena)* perennial, sometimes treated as annual; blue, purple, pink, red, white; summer–fall.

Watsonia *(Watsonia beatricis)* corm; orange-red; summer–fall.

Weigela *(Weigela)* shrub; red, white, pink, yellow; early summer, sometimes longer.

Wishbone flower *(Torenia fournieri)* annual; blue, purple, white; summer–fall.

Wisteria *(Wisteria)* vine; purple, blue, pink, white; late spring.

Yellow bells *(Tecoma stans)* shrub or small tree; yellow; June–January.

Yucca *(Yucca)* perennial, shrub, tree; white; late winter–late summer.

Zinnia *(Zinnia)* annual; various colors; summer–frost.

Wildflowers

Alum root, island *(Heuchera maxima)* white; February–April; southern California.

Basswood *(Tilia americana)* yellowish white; June–July; northeastern and midwestern U.S.

Beardtongue, foxglove *(Penstemon digitalis)* white; May–July; eastern U.S.

Bee balm *(Monarda didyma)* red; June–September; eastern U.S.

Bee balm, mintleaf *(Monarda menthifolia)* pinkish purple; May–August; southwestern U.S., Rocky Mountains.

Bee balm, plains *(Monarda pectinata)* whitish pink; May–September; Great Plains, southwestern U.S.

Bee plant, Rocky Mountain *(Cleome serrulata)* pink; May–September; western U.S.

Bergamot, wild *(Monarda fistulosa)* pinkish purple; June–September; eastern U.S.

Bladderpod *(Isomeris arborea)* yellow; most of year; southern California.

Bleeding heart, wild *(Dicentra eximia)* pink; April–September; eastern U.S., except extreme Southeast.

Bluebells, Virginia *(Mertensia virginica)* blue; March–June; eastern U.S.

Bluebonnet, Texas *(Lupinus texensis)* blue; March–May; Texas.

Bouncing bet *(Saponaria officinalis)* pinkish white; June–September; widespread across U.S.

Bouvardia, scarlet *(Bouvardia ternifolia)* red; May–November; southwestern U.S.

Buckeye, California *(Aesculus californica)* whitish pink; spring; California.

Buckeye, Ohio *(Aesculus glabra)* yellow; spring; midwestern U.S.

Buckeye, red *(Aesculus pavia)* red; spring; southeastern U.S.

Butterfly weed *(Asclepias tuberosa)* orange; April–September; most of U.S., except extreme West.

Buttonbush *(Cephalanthus occidentalis)* white; May–August; eastern U.S., southwestern U.S. to California.

Cactus, claret cup *(Echinocereus triglochidiatus)* red; April–July; southwestern U.S., Rocky Mountains.

California bell *(Phacelia minor)* purple; March–June; southern California.

California fuchsia, or hummingbird flower *(Zauschneria californica)* red; August–October; extreme southwestern U.S., California north to southwestern Oregon.

Cardinal flower *(Lobelia cardinalis)* red; May–December; most of U.S., except Northwest.

Catchfly, roundleaf *(Silene rotundifolia)* red; June–July; eastern U.S., except Northeast.

Catchfly, royal *(Silene regia)* red; June–August; eastern U.S., except Northeast.

Cholla, tree *(Opuntia imbricata)* pink; May–August; southwestern U.S.

Chuparosa *(Beloperone californica)* red; February–June; extreme southwestern U.S.

Columbine, barrel *(Aquilegia triternata)* red; May–October; southwestern U.S., Rocky Mountains.

Columbine, Colorado *(Aquilegia caerulea)* blue and white; June–August; Rocky Mountains, northern Southwest.

Columbine, crimson *(Aquilegia formosa)* red; April–August; western U.S., north to Alaska.

Columbine, golden *(Aquilegia chrysantha)* yellow; April–September; southwestern U.S., Rocky Mountains.

Columbine, wild *(Aquilegia canadensis)* red; March–July; eastern U.S., west to Texas.

Coral bean *(Erythrina herbacea)* red; March–July; southeastern U.S.

Coral bean, western *(Erythrina flabelliformis)* red; spring; extreme southwestern U.S.

Coral bells *(Heuchera sanguinea)* red; February–October; Arizona.

Coralberry *(Symphoricarpos orbiculatus)* purplish green; July–August; eastern U.S. from Rockies east.

Crevice heuchera *(Heuchera micrantha)* white; May–August; extreme western U.S.

Crimson woolly pod *(Astragalus coccineus)* red; March–June; extreme southwestern U.S.

Currant, golden *(Ribes odoratum)* yellow; April–June; midwestern U.S., Great Plains.

Currant, red-flowering *(Ribes sanguineum)* pink, red; March–June; northwestern U.S.

Delphinium, cañon *(Delphinium nudicaule)* red; March–June; California, southwestern Oregon.

Delphinium, scarlet *(Delphinium cardinale)* red; May–July; coastal California mountains, north to Monterey County.

Desert bell *(Phacelia campanularia)* blue; February–May; southern California.

Desert globemallow, or desert hollyhock *(Sphaeralcea ambigua)* orange-red, pink; March–June, sometimes longer; southwestern U.S.

Desert honeysuckle *(Anisacanthus thurberi)* orange; April–October; southwestern U.S.

Desert plume, or golden prince's plume *(Stanleya pinnata)* yellow; April–September; western U.S.

Desert willow *(Chilopsis linearis)* pink, white, purple; April–September; southwestern U.S.

Fairy duster *(Calliandra eriophylla)* pink; February–May; extreme southwestern U.S.

Figwort, California *(Scrophularia californica)* red-brown; February–August; extreme western U.S.

Firecracker, Eaton's *(Penstemon eatonii)* red; February–July; southwestern U.S., southwest Rocky Mountains.

Firecracker flower *(Dichelostemma ida-maia)* red; May–July; northwestern California, southwestern Oregon.

Fire pink *(Silene virginica)* red; April–June; eastern U.S.

Fireweed *(Epilobium angustifolium)* pink; June–September; widespread across U.S., except extreme Southeast.

Flame acanthus *(Anisacanthus wrightii)* red; June–July; Texas.

Four o'clock, mountain *(Mirabilis oblongifolia)* pink; June–October; southwestern U.S.

Geiger tree *(Cordia sebestena)* orange; year-round; extreme southern Florida.

Golden ear-drops *(Dicentra chrysantha)* yellow; April–September; central California south.

Gooseberry, fuchsia-flowering *(Ribes speciosum)* red; January–May; California.

Hedge nettle, California *(Stachys bullata)* pink; April–September; California.

Hedge nettle, great *(Stachys cooleyae)* pink; June–August; northwestern U.S.

Hedge nettle, whitestem *(Stachys albens)* white, pink; May–October; California.

Hibiscus *(Hibiscus coccineus)* red; June–September; extreme southeastern U.S.

Hibiscus, heartleaf *(Hibiscus cardiophyllus)* red; most of year; Texas.

Honeysuckle, fly *(Lonicera canadensis)* yellowish green; April–August; eastern U.S., except extreme Southeast.

Honeysuckle, four-lined *(Lonicera involucrata)* yellowish; June–July; northern U.S. to Alaska.

Honeysuckle, orange *(Lonicera ciliosa)* orange; May–July; northwestern U.S.

Honeysuckle, Tartarian *(Lonicera tatarica)* pink, white; May–June; northeastern U.S.

Honeysuckle, trumpet *(Lonicera sempervirens)* red; April–September; eastern U.S.

Hound's tongue *(Cynoglossum grande)* blue; March–July; southern California north to Washington.

Indian pink *(Spigelia marilandica)* red; March–October; southeastern U.S.

Indian pink, California *(Silene californica)* red; March–August; California, southern Oregon.

Indian warrior *(Pedicularis densiflora)* red; January–June; California, southern Oregon.

Jewelweed *(Impatiens capensis)* orange; July–October; most of U.S., except extreme Southwest.

Lily, Turk's-cap *(Lilium superbum)* orange; July–September; eastern U.S.

Locust, black *(Robinia pseudoacacia)* white; late spring–early summer; widespread across U.S.

Locust, New Mexico *(Robinia neomexicana)* pink; late spring–early summer; southwestern U.S.

Lousewort, dwarf *(Pedicularis semibarbata)* yellow; May–July; extreme western U.S., except extreme Northwest.

Macranthera flammea (No common name) orange; August–October; extreme southeastern U.S.

Macromeria, green-flowered *(Macromeria viridiflora)* greenish yellow; May–September; southwestern U.S.

Monardella, red *(Monardella macrantha)* red; June–August; central California south.

Monkeyflower, orange bush *(Mimulus aurantiacus)* orange; March–August; California, southwestern Oregon.

Monkeyflower, scarlet *(Mimulus cardinalis)* red; March–October; most of western U.S.

Morning glory, small red *(Ipomoea coccinea)* red; July–October; widespread across U.S., except Northwest.

Mountain laurel *(Kalmia latifolia)* pinkish white; May–July; eastern U.S.

Mountain pride *(Penstemon newberryi)* pink; June–August; central California north to southwestern Oregon.

Mountain rosebay *(Rhododendron catawbiense)* pink; May–June; southeastern U.S.

New Jersey tea *(Ceanothus americanus)* white; May–September; eastern U.S.

Ocotillo *(Fouquieria splendens)* red; spring–summer; southwestern U.S.

Paintbrush, desert *(Castilleja chromosa)* red; March–August; most of western U.S.

Paintbrush, giant red *(Castilleja miniata)* red; May–October; western U.S.

Paintbrush, Great Plains *(Castilleja sessiliflora)* pink; March–September; most of U.S. from Mississippi River west.

Paintbrush, Indian *(Castilleja coccinea)* red; May–July; eastern U.S.

Paintbrush, southwestern *(Castilleja integra)* red; March–October; southwestern U.S.

Penstemon, Arizona *(Penstemon pseudospectabilis)* red; February–May; southwestern U.S.

Penstemon, Bacchus's *(Penstemon baccharifolius)* red; April–September; western Texas.

Penstemon, cardinal *(Penstemon cardinalis)* red; May–July; extreme southwestern U.S.

Penstemon, cliff *(Penstemon rupicola)* pink; May–August; northwestern U.S.

Penstemon, golden-beard *(Penstemon barbatus)* red; June–October; southwestern U.S., Rocky Mountains.

Penstemon, Murray's *(Penstemon murrayanus)* red; April–May; most of eastern U.S., except Northeast.

Penstemon, Palmer's *(Penstemon palmeri)* pink; March–September; southwestern U.S.

Penstemon, Parry's *(Penstemon parryi)* pink; February–May; southern Arizona.

Penstemon, porch *(Penstemon strictus)* blue, purple; June–July; southwestern U.S., Rocky Mountains.

Penstemon, red shrubby *(Penstemon corymbosus)* red; June–October; northern California.

Penstemon, royal *(Penstemon spectabilis)* blue; April–June; southern California.

Penstemon, scarlet *(Penstemon labrosus)* red; July–August; southern California.

Phlox, wild blue *(Phlox divaricata)* blue; April–June; eastern U.S.

Pinxter flower *(Rhododendron nudiflorum)* pink; March–June; eastern U.S.

Redbud, eastern *(Cercis canadensis)* pink; spring; eastern U.S.

Redbud, western *(Cercis occidentalis)* pink; spring; California, southwestern U.S.

Sage, autumn *(Salvia greggii)* red; March–November; Texas.

Sage, crimson *(Salvia henryi)* red; April–September; extreme southwestern U.S.

Sage, Lemmon's *(Salvia lemmonii)* pink; July–October; southern Arizona.

Sage, mountain *(Salvia regla)* red; July–December; Texas.

Sage, pitcher, or hummingbird sage *(Salvia spathacea)* red; March–July; central California south.

Sage, scarlet *(Salvia coccinea)* red; March–frost; extreme southeastern U.S., west to Texas coast.

Scarlet bugler *(Penstemon centranthifolius)* red; April–July; central California south.

Scarletbush *(Hamelia patens)* red; year-round; extreme southern Florida.

Scarlet fritillary *(Fritillaria recurva)* red; March–July; central West Coast to western Nevada.

Scarlet gilia, or standing cypress *(Ipomopsis rubra)* red; May–September; southeastern U.S.

Showy rattlebox *(Crotolaria spectabilis)* yellow; August–October; southeastern U.S.

Skyrocket *(Ipomopsis aggregata)* red, pink; May–September; most of western U.S.

Snowberry *(Symphoricarpus albus)* pink; May–July; eastern U.S. from Rockies east.

Snow plant *(Sarcodes sanguinea)* red; April–July; extreme western U.S., except extreme Northwest.

Solomon's seal, great *(Polygonatum canaliculatum)* white; May–June; eastern U.S.

Swamp honeysuckle *(Rhododendron viscosum)* white; June–September; eastern U.S.

Texas betony *(Stachys coccinea)* red; March–October; extreme southwestern U.S.

Texas mallow *(Malvaviscus arboreus)* red; year-round; extreme southeastern U.S., west to Texas.

Texas silverleaf *(Leucophyllum frutescens)* pink; June–November; southern Texas.

Thistle *(Cirsium)* red, pink, purple, yellow, white; March–October; widespread across U.S.

Trumpet creeper, or trumpet flower *(Campsis radicans)* orange-red; July–September; eastern U.S.

Turtlehead *(Chelone glabra)* white, pink; July–October; eastern U.S.

Wallflower, Menzies's *(Erysimum menziesii)* yellow; March–May; coastal California.

Wallflower, western *(Erysimum capitatum)* orange, yellow; February–September; western U.S.

Wild pine *(Tillandsia fasciculata)* red; January–August; Florida.

Wood betony, or lousewort *(Pedicularis canadensis)* red, yellow, red and yellow; March–July; most of U.S. from Rocky Mountains east.

Woolly blue curls *(Trichostema lanatum)* blue; April–August, sometimes longer; California.

Where to
Get Plants

In addition to local and mail-order nurseries that carry regular garden plants, you can obtain hummingbird plants from the following sources.

Hummingbird Gardens
P.O. Box 225
La Honda, CA 94020
Send self-addressed stamped envelope for plant list.

Nursery Sources: Native Plants and Wildflowers
Booklet available from the New England Wild Flower Society, Garden in the Woods, Hemenway Road, Framingham,

MA 01701. Contains listings of native plant nurseries for most states. ($6.95 postpaid)

Sources of Native Seeds and Plants
Booklet available from the Soil and Water Conservation Society of America, 7515 Northeast Ankeny Road, Ankeny, IA 50021. Contains listings of native plant nurseries for most states. ($3.00 postpaid)

Where to Get Hummingbird Feeders

~·~

You can obtain hummingbird feeders by mail order from the following sources.

Audubon Workshop
1501 Paddock Drive
Northbrook, IL 60062

BackYard Birds & Co.
717 South Broadview Drive
Springfield, MO 65809

The Barn Owl Gift Shop
2509 Lakeshore Drive
Fennville, MI 49408

The Brown Company
Yawgoo Pond Road
P.O. Box 277
West Kingston, RI 02892

Burd Corporation
P.O. Box 580
Cedaredge, CO 81413

Droll Yankees
27 Mill Road
Foster, RI 02825

Duncraft
Penacook, NH 03303

Heath Manufacturing Company
P.O. Box 105
Coopersville, MI 49404

Hummingbird Heaven
1255 Carmel Drive
Simi Valley, CA 93065

Hyde Bird Feeder Company
56 Felton Street
P.O. Box 168
Waltham, MA 02254

The Nature Company
P.O. Box 2310
Berkeley, CA 94702

North States Industries
1200 Mendelssohn Avenue
Suite 210
Minneapolis, MN 55427

Opus
24 William Way
P.O. Box 525
Bellingham, MA 02019

Perky-Pet Products
2201 South Wabash Street
Denver, CO 80231

Wild Birds Unlimited
1430 Broad Ripple Avenue
Indianapolis, IN 46220

Ornithological and Wildlife Conservation Organizations

American Birding Association
P.O. Box 6599
Colorado Springs, CO 80934

American Ornithologists' Union
National Museum of Natural History
Smithsonian Institution
Washington, D.C. 20560

Association of Field
Ornithologists
Manomet Bird Observatory
P.O. Box 936
Manomet, MA 02345

Cooper Ornithological Society
Department of Biology
University of California
Los Angeles, CA 90024

Cornell Laboratory of
Ornithology
159 Sapsucker Woods Road
Ithaca, NY 14850

International Council for Bird
Preservation
United States Section
801 Pennsylvania Avenue, S.E.
Washington, D.C. 20003

National Audubon Society
950 Third Avenue
New York, NY 10022

National Wildlife Federation
1400 Sixteenth Street, N.W.
Washington, D.C. 20036

Organization for Tropical Studies
North American Headquarters
P.O. Box DM
Duke Station
Durham, NC 27706

Wilson Ornithological Society
Museum of Zoology
University of Michigan
Ann Arbor, MI 48109

World Wildlife Fund
1250 24th Street, N.W.
Washington, D.C. 20037

Wildflower, Native Plant, and Gardening Organizations

American Association of Botanical
  Gardens and Arboreta
P.O. Box 206
Swarthmore, PA 19081

American Forestry Association
P.O. Box 2000
Washington, D.C. 20013

American Horticultural Society
P.O. Box 0105
Mount Vernon, VA 22121

The Garden Club of America
598 Madison Avenue
New York, NY 10022

National Council of State
  Garden Clubs
4401 Magnolia Avenue
St. Louis, MO 63110

National Gardening Association
180 Flynn Avenue
Burlington, VT 05401

National Wildflower Research
  Center
2600 FM 973 North
Austin, TX 78725

"Botanical Clubs and Native Plant Societies of the United States," a list available for
$1.75 postpaid from the New England Wild Flower Society, Garden in the Woods,
Hemenway Road, Framingham, MA 01701. Contains listings for most states.

Bibliography

Hummingbirds

Allen, Arthur A. "A New Light Dawns on Bird Photography." *National Geographic,* June 1948.

American Forestry Association. "Tropical Deforestation: Why Is It Happening?" (pull-out poster). *American Forests,* November/December 1988.

American Ornithologists' Union. *Check-list of North American Birds.* 6th ed. Lawrence, Kansas: American Ornithologists' Union, 1983.

Armstrong, Robert H. *A Guide to the Birds of Alaska.* Anchorage: Alaska Northwest Publishing Co., 1980.

Audubon, John James. *Ornithological Biography.* Edinburgh: Adam Black, 1831.

———. *The Birds of America.* New York: Macmillan Co., 1937.

———. *The Birds of America.* Vol. 4. New York: Dover Publications, 1967.

Austin, Daniel F. "Bird Flowers in the Eastern United States." *Florida Scientist* 38(1975):1–12.

Baptista, Luis F., and Matsui, Margaret. "The Source of the Dive-Noise of the Anna's Hummingbird." *Condor* 81(1979):87–89.

Bassett, Frank N. "The Nuptial Flight of the Allen Hummingbird." *Condor* 23(1921):37.

———. "The Bathing of Hummingbirds." *Condor* 24(1922):63–64.

———. "The Anna Hummingbird Takes a Shower Bath." *Condor* 26(1924):227.

Bené, Frank. "Experiments on the Color Preference of Black-chinned Hummingbirds." *Condor* 43(1941):237–242.

————. "The Role of Learning in the Feeding Behavior of Black-chinned Hummingbirds." *Condor* 47(1945):3–22.

————. *The Feeding and Related Behavior of Hummingbirds with Special Reference to the Black-chin,* Archilochus alexandri *(Bourcier and Mulsant).* Memoirs of the Boston Society of Natural History, vol. 9, pp. 395–478. Boston: Charles T. Branford Co., 1947.

Bent, Arthur Cleveland. *Life Histories of North American Cuckoos, Goatsuckers, Hummingbirds, and Their Allies.* United States National Museum Bulletin no. 176, 1940. Reprint. New York: Dover Publications, 1989.

The Birds Around Us. San Francisco: Ortho Books, 1986.

Browning, Norma Lee, and Ogg, Russell. *He Saw a Hummingbird.* New York: E. P. Dutton, 1978.

Bull, John, and Farrand, John, Jr. *The Audubon Society Field Guide to North American Birds: Eastern Region.* New York: Alfred A. Knopf, 1977.

Carpenter, Bob. "Hummingbirds, Hummingbirds, Hummingbirds!" *WildBird,* September/October 1987.

Collar, N. J., and Andrew, P. *Birds to Watch: The ICBP World Checklist of Threatened Birds.* Technical pub. no. 8. Cambridge: International Council for Bird Preservation, Washington, D.C.: Smithsonian Institution Press, 1988.

Davis, William A., and Russell, Stephen M. *Birds in Southeastern Arizona.* 2d ed. Tucson: Tucson Audubon Society, 1984.

DeBenedictis, Paul. "Allen's and Rufous Hummingbirds." *Birding,* July/August 1976.

Diamond, A. W., and Lovejoy, T. E., eds. *Conservation of Tropical Forest Birds.* Technical pub. no. 4. Cambridge: International Council for Bird Preservation, 1985.

Dickey, Florence Van Vechten. *Familiar Birds of the Pacific Southwest.* Stanford, Calif.: Stanford University Press, 1935.

Doughty, Robin W. *Feather Fashions and Bird Preservation: A Study in Nature Protection.* Berkeley and Los Angeles: University of California Press, 1975.

Edgerton, Harold E. "Hummingbirds in Action." *National Geographic,* August 1947.

Edgerton, Harold E.; Niedrach, R. J.; and Riper, Walker Van. "Freezing the Flight of Hummingbirds." *National Geographic,* August 1951.

Edwards, Ernest Preston. *Finding Birds in Mexico.* 2d ed. Sweet Briar, Va.: Ernest P. Edwards, 1968.

————. *1985 Supplement to Finding Birds in Mexico (1968).* Sweet Briar, Va.: Ernest P. Edwards, 1985.

————. *A Field Guide to the Birds of Mexico.* 2d ed. Sweet Briar, Va.: Ernest P. Edwards, 1989.

Ehrlich, Paul R.; Dobkin, David S.; and Wheye, Darryl. *The Birder's Handbook: A Field Guide to the Natural History of North American Birds.* New York: Simon & Schuster, 1988.

Ewald, Paul W. "Hummingbirds: The Nectar Connection." *National Geographic,* February 1982.

Farrand, John, Jr. *Eastern Birds.* New York: McGraw-Hill, 1988.

————. *Western Birds.* New York: McGraw-Hill, 1988.

Feduccia, Alan, ed. *Catesby's Birds of Colonial America.* Chapel Hill: University of North Carolina Press, 1985.

Feinsinger, Peter. "The Long and Short of Hummingbird Bills." *International Wildlife,* July/August 1988.

Garrett, Kimball, and Dunn, Jon. *Birds of Southern California: Status and Distribution.* Los Angeles: Los Angeles Audubon Society, 1981.

Grant, Karen A., and Grant, Verne. *Hummingbirds and Their Flowers.* New York: Columbia University Press, 1968.

Greenewalt, Crawford H. "The Hummingbirds." *National Geographic,* November 1960.

————. *Hummingbirds.* Garden City: Doubleday & Co., 1960.

————. "Photographing Hummingbirds in Brazil." *National Geographic,* January 1963.

————. "The Marvelous Hummingbird Rediscovered." *National Geographic,* July 1966.

Greenway, James C., Jr. *Extinct and Vanishing Birds of the World.* 2d rev. ed. New York: Dover Publications, 1967.

Gross, Marguerite. "Display's the Thing." *Bird Watcher's Digest,* May/June 1985.

Grzimek, Bernard, ed. *Grzimek's Animal Life Encyclopedia.* Vol. 8. New York: Van Nostrand Reinhold Co., 1972.

Harrison, Hal H. *A Field Guide to Birds' Nests.* Boston: Houghton Mifflin Co., 1975.

————. *A Field Guide to Western Birds' Nests.* Boston: Houghton Mifflin Co., 1979.

Hinman, D. A. "Habits of the Ruby-throated Hummingbird." *Auk* 45(1928):504–505.

Hoagland, Edward. "Nectar Feeding." *The Nation,* July 20/27, 1985.

James, Robert Leslie. "Some Hummingbird Flowers East of the Mississippi." *Castanea* 13(1948):97–109.

Johnsgard, Paul A. *The Hummingbirds of North America.* Washington, D.C.: Smithsonian Institution Press, 1983.

————. *Birds of the Rocky Mountains.* Boulder: Colorado Associated University Press, 1986.

Kilham, Lawrence. *On Watching Birds*. Chelsea, Vermont: Chelsea Green Publishing Co., 1988.

Kress, Stephen W. *The Audubon Society Handbook for Birders*. New York: Charles Scribner's Sons, 1981.

Lawson, John. *A New Voyage to Carolina*. Chapel Hill: University of North Carolina Press, 1967.

Legg, Ken, and Pitelka, Frank A. "Ecological Overlap of Allen and Anna Hummingbirds Nesting at Santa Cruz, California." *Condor* 58(1956):393–405.

Levy, Seymour H. "A Possible United States Breeding Area for the Violet-crowned Hummingbird." *Auk* 75(1958):350.

Lincoln, F. C. "Some Notes of the Birds of Rock Canyon, Arizona." *Wilson Bulletin* 29(1917):65–73.

Lyerly, Samuel B.; Riess, Bernard F.; and Ross, Sherman. "Color Preference in the Mexican Violet-eared Hummingbird, *Calibri t. Thalassinus* (Swainson)." *Behaviour* 2(1950):237–248.

Marden, Luis. "The Man Who Talks to Hummingbirds." *National Geographic*, January 1963.

Miller, Millie, and Nelson, Cyndi. *Hummers: Hummingbirds of North America*. Boulder: Johnson Books, 1987.

Monson, Gale, and Phillips, Allan R. *Annotated Checklist of the Birds of Arizona*. 2d ed. Tucson: University of Arizona Press, 1981.

National Geographic Society. *Field Guide to the Birds of North America*. 2d ed. Washington, D.C.: National Geographic Society, 1987.

Pasquier, Roger F. *Watching Birds: An Introduction to Ornithology*. Boston: Houghton Mifflin Co., 1977.

Pearson, Oliver P. "The Daily Energy Requirements of a Wild Anna Hummingbird." *Condor* 56(1954):317–322.

Peterson, Roger Tory. *A Field Guide to the Birds of Texas*. Boston: Houghton Mifflin Co., 1963.

————. *Birds Over America*. Rev. ed. New York: Dodd, Mead & Co., 1964.

————. *A Field Guide to the Birds*. 4th ed. Boston: Houghton Mifflin Co., 1980.

————. *A Field Guide to Western Birds*. 3d ed. Boston: Houghton Mifflin Co., 1990.

Peterson, Roger Tory, and Chalif, Edward L. *A Field Guide to Mexican Birds*. Boston: Houghton Mifflin Co., 1973.

Phillips, Allan R. "The Migrations of Allen's and Other Hummingbirds." *Condor* 77(1975):196–205.

Phillips, Allan; Marshall, Joe; and Monson, Gale. *The Birds of Arizona*. Tucson: University of Arizona Press, 1964.

Pickens, Andrew L. "Unique Method of Pollination by the Ruby-throat." *Auk* 44(1927):24–27.

————. "Favorite Colors of Hummingbirds." *Auk* 47(1930):346–352.

————. "A Red Figwort as the Ideal Nearctic Bird-Flower." *Condor* 43(1941):100–102.

————. "Seasonal Territory Studies of Ruby-throats." *Auk* 61(1944):88–92.

Pitelka, Frank A. "Territoriality and Related Problems in North American Hummingbirds." *Condor* 44(1942):189–204.

Rappole, John H., and Blacklock, Gene W. *Birds of the Texas Coastal Bend: Abundance and Distribution.* College Station: Texas A&M University Press, 1985.

Ray, Rose Carolyn. "Discovery of a Nest and Eggs of the Blue-throated Hummingbird." *Condor* 27(1925):49–51.

Reed, Chester A. *North American Birds Eggs.* Rev. ed. New York: Dover Publications, 1965.

Ridgway, Robert. "The Humming Birds." In *Report of the U.S. National Museum* (for 1890), pp. 253–383. Washington: Government Printing Office, 1891.

Robbins, Chandler S.; Bruun, Bertel; and Zim, Herbert S. *Birds of North America.* Rev. ed. New York: Golden Press, 1983.

Skutch, Alexander F. *The Life of the Hummingbird.* New York: Crown Publishers, 1973.

————. *A Bird Watcher's Adventures in Tropical America.* Austin: University of Texas Press, 1977.

Small, Arnold. *The Birds of California.* New York: Winchester Press, 1974.

Stiles, F. Gary. *Food Supply and the Annual Cycle of the Anna Hummingbird.* University of California Publications in Zoology, vol. 97, pp. 1–109. Berkeley and Los Angeles: University of California Press, 1973.

————. "Taste Preferences, Color Preferences, and Flower Choice in Hummingbirds." *Condor* 78(1976):10–26.

————. "Altitudinal Movements of Birds on the Caribbean Slope of Costa Rica: Implications for Conservation." In Almeda, Frank, and Pringle, Catherine M., eds. *Tropical Rainforests: Diversity and Conservation.* San Francisco: California Academy of Sciences and Pacific Division, American Association for the Advancement of Science, 1988.

Sutton, George Miksch. *At a Bend in a Mexican River.* New York: Paul S. Eriksson, 1972.

————. *Birds Worth Watching.* Norman: University of Oklahoma Press, 1986.

Taverner, P. A., and Swales, B. H. "The Birds of Point Pelee." *Wilson Bulletin* 19(1907):133–153.

Terres, John K. *Flashing Wings: The Drama of Bird Flight.* Garden City: Doubleday & Co., 1968.

Tyrrell, Esther Quesada, and Tyrrell, Robert A. *Hummingbirds: Their Life and Behavior.* New York: Crown Publishers, 1985.

————. *Hummingbirds of the Caribbean.* New York: Crown Publishers, 1990.

Udvardy, Miklos D. F. *The Audubon Society Field Guide to North American Birds: Western Region*. New York: Alfred A. Knopf, 1977.

Unitt, Philip. *The Birds of San Diego County*. San Diego: San Diego Society of Natural History, 1984.

Wetmore, Alexander. "Seeking the Smallest Feathered Creatures." *National Geographic*, July 1932.

Weymouth, Robert D.; Lasiewski, Robert C.; and Berger, Andrew J. "The Tongue Apparatus in Hummingbirds." *Acta Anatomica* 58(1964):252–270.

Winthrop, John. "A Further Accompt of the Stellar Fish; Formerly Described in Numb. 57. p. 1153; With the Addition of Some Other Curiosities." *Philosophical Transactions* 6(1671):2221–2224.

Woods, Robert S. "The Hummingbirds of California." *Auk* 44(1927):297–318.

Yule, Lauray. "Hummingbirds." *Tucson Guide Quarterly*, Winter 1988.

Zim, Herbert S., and Gabrielson, Ira N. *Birds*. Rev. ed. New York: Golden Press, 1987.

Hummingbird Gardening

Arbib, Robert, and Soper, Tony. *The Hungry Bird Book*. New York: Taplinger Publishing Co., 1971.

Arnold, Nancy E. "The Day of the Hummingbird." *Illinois Audubon*, Fall 1988.

Attracting Birds to Your Garden. Menlo Park, Calif.: Lane Books, 1974.

Bodine, Margaret L. "Holidays With Humming Birds." *National Geographic*, June 1928.

Brown, Vinson. *Backyard Wild Birds of California and the Pacific Northwest*. Jersey City: T.F.H. Publications, 1965.

Damrosch, Barbara. *Theme Gardens*. New York: Workman Publishing Co., 1982.

Davison, Verne E. *Attracting Birds: from the Prairies to the Atlantic*. New York: Thomas Y. Crowell, 1967.

Dennis, John V. *A Complete Guide to Bird Feeding*. New York: Alfred A. Knopf, 1975.

————. *The Wildlife Gardener*. New York: Alfred A. Knopf, 1985.

Dennis, John V., and Murphy, Pat. "A BWD Hummingbird Survey." *Bird Watcher's Digest*, September/October 1983.

————. "A BWD Report: Feeding Hummingbirds." *Bird Watcher's Digest*, May/June 1984.

Dimmitt, Mark. "Landscaping For (and Against) Wildlife." *sonorensis*, Winter 1989.

Ernst, Ruth Shaw. *The Naturalist's Garden*. Emmaus, Pa.: Rodale Press, 1987.

Harrison, George H. *The Backyard Bird Watcher*. New York: Simon & Schuster, 1979.

————. "How to Attract Hummingbirds." *National Wildlife,* April/May 1985.

Holmgren, Virginia C. *The Way of the Hummingbird.* Santa Barbara: Capra Press, 1986.

How to Attract Birds. San Francisco: Ortho Books, 1983.

Kress, Stephen W. *The Audubon Society Guide to Attracting Birds.* New York: Charles Scribner's Sons, 1985.

McElroy, Thomas P., Jr. *The New Handbook of Attracting Birds.* 2d ed. New York: Alfred A. Knopf, 1960.

Mason, C. Russell. "Invite Hummingbirds to Your Garden." *The Bulletin of the Massachusetts Audubon Society* 39(1955):217–221.

Murphy, Pat, and Dennis, John V. "Attracting & Feeding Hummingbirds: Second Report." *Bird Watcher's Digest,* May/June 1985.

Newfield, Nancy L. "Plant a Hummingbird Garden." *Birder's World,* March/April 1987.

Newsom-Brighton, Maryanne. "A Garden Fit for Hummingbirds." *Horticulture,* February 1986.

Pickens, A. L., and Garrison, Lura P. "Two-Year Record of the Ruby-throat's Visits to a Garden." *Auk* 48(1931):532–537.

Pistorius, Alan. *The Country Journal Book of Birding and Bird Attraction.* New York: W. W. Norton & Co., 1981.

Sherman, Althea R. "Experiments in Feeding Hummingbirds During Seven Summers." *Wilson Bulletin* 25(1913):153–166.

Soule, Caroline G. "A Hummingbird Experiment." *Bird-Lore* 2(1900):158.

Spofford, Sally Hoyt. "Some Sticky Solutions." *The Living Bird Quarterly,* Spring 1985.

Stuart-Smith, Margaret. "Hummers at Our Feeders." *WildBird,* June 1987.

Terres, John K. *Songbirds in Your Garden.* 3d ed. New York: Hawthorn Books, 1977.

Tufts, Craig. *The Backyard Naturalist.* Washington, D.C.: National Wildlife Federation, 1988.

Flowers and Gardening

African Violets and Other Flowering Houseplants. San Francisco: Ortho Books, 1985.

All About Annuals. San Francisco: Ortho Books, 1981.

All About Azaleas, Camellias & Rhododendrons. San Francisco: Ortho Books, 1985.

All About Bulbs. Rev. ed. San Francisco: Ortho Books, 1986.

All About Citrus & Subtropical Fruits. San Francisco: Ortho Books, 1985.

All About Growing Fruits, Berries & Nuts. San Francisco: Ortho Books, 1987.

All About Houseplants. San Francisco: Ortho Books, 1982.

All About Perennials. San Francisco: Ortho Books, 1981.

Beckett, Kenneth A.; Carr, David; and Stevens, David. *The Contained Garden.* New York: The Viking Press, 1983.

Bianchini, Francesco, and Pantano, Azzurra Carrasa. *Simon & Schuster's Guide to Plants and Flowers.* New York: Simon & Schuster, 1974.

Brockman, C. Frank. *Trees of North America.* New York: Golden Press, 1979.

Chiusoli, Alessandro, and Boriani, Maria Luisa. *Simon & Schuster's Guide to House Plants.* New York: Simon & Schuster, 1986.

Container Gardening. Menlo Park, Calif.: Lane Publishing Co., 1984.

Craighead, John J.; Craighead, Frank C., Jr.; and Davis, Ray J. *A Field Guide to Rocky Mountain Wildflowers.* Boston: Houghton Mifflin Co., 1963.

Elias, Thomas S. *The Complete Trees of North America: Field Guide and Natural History.* New York: Van Nostrand Reinhold Co., 1980.

Evans, Hazel. *The Patio Garden.* New York: Penguin Books, 1986.

Everett, Thomas H. *The New York Botanical Garden Illustrated Encyclopedia of Horticulture.* 10 vols. New York: Garland Publishing, 1980–82.

Garden Color: Annuals & Perennials. Menlo Park, Calif.: Lane Publishing Co., 1981.

Gardening in Containers. Rev. ed. San Francisco: Ortho Books, 1983.

Hortus Third: A Concise Dictionary of Plants Cultivated in the United States and Canada. New York: Macmillan Co., 1976.

How to Select & Care for Shrubs & Hedges. San Francisco: Ortho Books, 1980.

Ideas for Hanging Gardens. Menlo Park, Calif.: Lane Publishing Co., 1974.

Kotarski, Georgiana C. "Pineapple Sage." *Flower and Garden,* June/July 1986.

Landscaping for Privacy. Menlo Park, Calif.: Lane Publishing Co., 1985.

Landscaping with Wildflowers & Native Plants. San Francisco: Ortho Books, 1984.

Little, Elbert L. *The Audubon Society Field Guide to North American Trees: Eastern Region.* New York: Alfred A. Knopf, 1980.

————. *The Audubon Society Field Guide to North American Trees: Western Region.* New York: Alfred A. Knopf, 1980.

Loughmiller, Campbell and Lynn. *Texas Wildflowers: A Field Guide.* Austin: University of Texas Press, 1984.

Lunardi, Costanza. *Simon & Schuster's Guide to Shrubs and Vines and Other Small Ornamentals.* New York: Simon & Schuster, 1988.

Moggi, Guido, and Giugnolini, Luciano. *Simon & Schuster's Guide to Garden Flowers.* New York: Simon & Schuster, 1983.

Munz, Philip A. *A Flora of Southern California.* Berkeley and Los Angeles: University of California Press, 1974.

Munz, Philip A., and Keck, David D. *A California Flora.* Berkeley and Los Angeles: University of California Press, 1959.

National Wildflower Research Center. *The National Wildflower Research Center's Wildflower Handbook.* Austin: Texas Monthly Press, 1989.

Niehaus, Theodore F., and Ripper, Charles L. *A Field Guide to Pacific States Wildflowers.* Boston: Houghton Mifflin Co., 1976.

Niehaus, Theodore F.; Ripper, Charles L.; and Savage, Virginia. *A Field Guide to Southwestern and Texas Wildflowers.* Boston: Houghton Mifflin Co., 1984.

Niering, William A., and Olmstead, Nancy C. *The Audubon Society Field Guide to North American Wildflowers: Eastern Region.* New York: Alfred A. Knopf, 1979.

Peterson, Roger Tory, and McKenny, Margaret. *A Field Guide to Wildflowers.* Boston: Houghton Mifflin Co., 1968.

Petrides, George A. *A Field Guide to Trees and Shrubs.* 2d ed. Boston: Houghton Mifflin Co., 1972.

Pizzetti, Mariella. *Simon & Schuster's Guide to Cacti and Succulents.* New York: Simon & Schuster, 1985.

Proctor, Michael, and Yeo, Peter. *The Pollination of Flowers.* New York: Taplinger Publishing Co., 1972.

Rickett, Harold William. *The New Field Book of American Wild Flowers.* New York: G. P. Putnam's Sons, 1963.

———. *Wild Flowers of the United States.* 6 vols. New York: McGraw-Hill, 1966–73.

Schmidt, Marjorie G. *Growing California Native Plants.* Berkeley and Los Angeles: University of California Press, 1980.

Shaw, William W. "Urban Conservation: Is It Feasible?" *sonorensis,* Winter 1989.

Siminski, Peter. "Wildlife in the Suburban Ecotone." *sonorensis,* Winter 1989.

Simon & Schuster's Guide to Trees. New York: Simon & Schuster, 1978.

Spellenberg, Richard. *The Audubon Society Field Guide to North American Wildflowers: Western Region.* New York: Alfred A. Knopf, 1979.

Stone, Doris M. *The Lives of Plants.* New York: Charles Scribner's Sons, 1983.

Taylor's Guide to Annuals. Boston: Houghton Mifflin Co., 1986.

Taylor's Guide to Bulbs. Boston: Houghton Mifflin Co., 1986.

Taylor's Guide to Perennials. Boston: Houghton Mifflin Co., 1986.

Taylor's Guide to Ground Covers, Vines & Grasses. Boston: Houghton Mifflin Co., 1987.

Taylor's Guide to Houseplants. Boston: Houghton Mifflin Co., 1987.

Taylor's Guide to Shrubs. Boston: Houghton Mifflin Co., 1987.

Taylor's Guide to Trees. Boston: Houghton Mifflin Co., 1988.

Venning, Frank D. *Wildflowers of North America*. New York: Golden Press, 1984.

Western Garden Book. Menlo Park, Calif.: Lane Publishing Co., 1988.

Wright, Michael. *The Complete Handbook of Garden Plants*. New York: Facts on File, 1984.

Wyman, Donald. *Shrubs and Vines for American Gardens*. Rev. ed. New York: Macmillan Co., 1969.

Zim, Herbert S., and Martin, Alexander C. *Flowers*. Rev. ed. New York: Golden Press, 1987.

Index